Book of Roman Decadence
Emperors of Debauchery

Edited by Geoffrey Farrington
and translated by Brian & Adrian Murdoch

Dedalus/Hippocrene

Supported by the Eastern Arts Board

Published in the UK by Dedalus Ltd, Langford Lodge, St Judith's Lane, Sawtry, Cambs, PE17 5XE

ISBN 1 873982 16 X

Published in the USA by Hippocrene Books Inc, 171, Madison Avenue, New York, NY 10016

Distributed in Canada by Marginal Distribution, Unit 103, 277, George Street North, Peterborough, Ontario, KJ9 3G9

Distributed in Australia & New Zealand by Peribo Pty Ltd, 26, Tepko Road, Terrey Hill, N.S.W. 2084

Distributed in South Africa by William Waterman Publications Limited P. O. Box 5091, Rivonia 2128

First published by Dedalus in 1994

Compilation & Introduction copyright © Geoffrey Farrington 1994
Original translations copyright © Brian & Adrian Murdoch

Printed in Finland by Wsoy
Typeset by Datix International Limited, Bungay, Suffolk

A C.I.P. listing for this title is available on request

Decadence from Dedalus

Titles in the Decadence from Dedalus series include:

Sense (and other stories) – Boito £6.99
The Child of Pleasure – D'Annunzio £7.99
The Triumph of Death – D'Annunzio £7.99
The Victim (L'Innocente) – D'Annunzio £7.99
Angels of Perversity – de Gourmont £6.99
The Dedalus Book of Roman Decadence – editor G. Farrington £7.99
The Dedalus Book of German Decadence –editor R. Furness (June 94) £8.99
La-Bas – J. K. Huysmans £7.99
Monsieur de Phocas – Lorrain £7.99
The Green Face – Meyrink £7.99
The Diary of a Chambermaid – Mirbeau £7.99
Torture Garden – Mirbeau £7.99
Le Calvaire – Mirbeau £7.99 (June 94)
Monsieur Venus – Rachilde £6.99
La Marquise de Sade – Rachilde £8.99 (August 94)
The Dedalus Book of Decadence – editor B. Stableford £7.99
The Second Dedalus Book of Decadence – editor B. Stableford £8.99

Decadent titles in the Dedalus European Classics series include:

Little Angel – Andreyev £4.95
The Red Laugh – Andreyev £4.95
Les Diaboliques – Barbey D'Aurevilly £6.99
The Cathedral – J. K. Huysmans £6.95
En Route – J. K. Huysmans £6.95

All these titles can be obtained from your local bookshop, or by post from Dedalus by writing to:
Dedalus Cash Sales, Langford Lodge, St Judith's Lane, Sawtry, Cambs, PE17 5XE
Please enclose a cheque to the value of the books ordered + £1 pp for the first book and 75p thereafter up to a maximum of £4.75

Contents

(Unless stated otherwise all the translations are by either Brian or Adrian Murdoch)

THE EDITOR

Geoffrey Farrington was born in London in 1955. After drama school he worked as a scriptwriter and performer in theatre, radio and television, along with helping to run the family business in South London. He is the author of a decadent novel set in the reign of Nero, *The Acts of the Apostates* (Dedalus 1990), and a vampire novel, *The Revenants* (Dedalus 1984).

THE TRANSLATORS

Adrian Murdoch was educated in Scotland and at the Queen's College, Oxford. After graduation he taught in Berlin for a year, working as well for the Ministry of Education as a translator and interpreter. He now works as a journalist in London.

Brian Murdoch studied at Exeter University and at Jesus College, Cambridge, and is currently Professor of German at Stirling University. He has published a large number of books and articles on medieval (and modern) Germanic, Celtic (especially Cornish) and comparative literature, as well as translations of medieval Latin and German epics. He is currently editing the *Dedalus Book of Medieval Decadence*, which will appear in 1995.

INTRODUCTION

Throughout history nothing has been more synonymous with decadence than imperial Rome. There are a good many reasons for this – aside from hackneyed images of gladiatorial combats and orgies – and foremost among them are probably the Roman emperors themselves. Certainly these men held more personal power than any other individuals in history, but the unique tradition and history of Rome meant that their power was very fiercely resented.

Rome grew from a small, monarchic city state, expelling the last of its Etruscan kings, the tyrannical Tarquinius Superbus, in the sixth century BC, and founding a republican system (or more accurately an oligarchical system) whose dubious concept of freedom became ingrained within its citizens as their greatest pride. This pride, and the dedication it engendered, did much to raise Rome to its eventual imperial glory, but the political system which guided Rome to greatness became finally the victim of its own success; citizens voting and senators debating was a method of government wholly inadequate to rule a world empire. And with empire came wealth, and with wealth ever greater corruption. Numerous upheavals among members of the leading Roman families as they vied for position and advantage led ultimately to civil war and the irrevocable collapse of the republican system.

The dictator Julius Caesar – granted special authority at a time of emergency – despite his contrived and ostentatious refusal of the title 'king', was assassinated on the Ides of March in 44 BC by those men faithful to the republican ideal who saw that Caesar aimed at kingship in all but the hated title (Caesar's own title of perpetual dictator would seem similarly odious to modern ears) but who also believed that his assassination would be sufficient to save the republic. This was tantamount to supposing that Caesar, his body lacerated by twenty-three stab wounds, might be revived by artificial respiration.

But the lesson to Caesar's adopted son and heir, his grandnephew Octavian (later the Emperor Augustus) was clear. The Romans – more specifically the Roman nobles – would not yet accept a ruler outright. A less flamboyant figure than Caesar, but no less ambitious (it is historically astonishing that two such different but remarkable men should have risen in succession to combine their abilities in such a monumental undertaking), Augustus set about painstakingly imposing his own solution to the problem. Having delivered Rome finally from the turmoil of civil war, and defeated at the naval battle of Actium his once colleague and later rival, Caesar's lieutenant Mark Antony in his alliance with Queen Cleopatra of Egypt, Augustus declared himself 'Imperator' (supreme military commander) from which the title 'emperor' was to derive and 'Princeps' (first citizen), who exceeded others not in power but in authority (Augustus' own words). To which any astute senator might have replied: 'Yes. And I am the Queen of Parthia's aunt Betty.'

Through a facade of empty republican traditions and titles, Augustus used this 'authority' to rule absolutely for forty years, and to pass on his powers to his chosen successor, his stepson Tiberius, when he died.

As time passed the pretence naturally wore thinner as subsequent emperors – particularly Caligula and Nero – became ever less discreet about cloaking the reality of their power. They were, of course, greatly resented by those senators, members of the old nobility whose forbears had survived the ruthless proscriptions upon their number by Augustus after the civil wars, and whose ancestral power and authority the emperors had usurped. They might still achieve the great republican offices of state – become quaestors, aediles, praetors and ultimately consuls – but these titles were finally little more than mere honours. All true promotion and advancement lay in the hands of the emperor. Political impotence bred indignation, and a nostalgia for the republican system, whose instabilities and impracticality these later generations had never experienced. Conspiracies against emperors became commonplace, and so consequently did the executions of those among the nobility whom emperors mistrusted. This frequently was most of them, given the enmity that grew between emperors and senate, and the progressive exclusion of senators from all real areas of power. The purges were particularly fierce within the imperial family itself. Every emperor after Augustus regarded his relatives as his closest potential rivals, and a likely focus for malcontents and conspirators; as indeed they often were. When Nero died in 68 AD the once abundant line of Augustus became extinct.

The humbler citizens of Rome, meanwhile suffering from an ever increasing chasm between rich and poor, and denied much gainful occupation in a slave-rich society, had declined into an ominous underclass, a mob whom the emperors must divert and placate constantly with 'bread and circuses'. Yet the imperial system brought with it a stability, peace and prosperity unknown in former times. Rome became a magnet and a melting pot for many diverse cultures. Luxuries from across the world flooded into its markets. It is hard to see how in such circumstances a decadent society might not have flourished. In the past the Romans had been a crude and pragmatic people — essentially soldiers and farmers — the inhabitants of a small city state which struggled for its right to survive against initially larger and more powerful neighbours. To increase and protect their city, to raise large families and work their fields, to form an ordered society and create stability and law: these are imperatives that allow little time for the development of sophisticated culture, for art or philosophy; little chance also for sexual activities to be directed at much beyond procreation. Thus in the early history of Rome we find none of the influence of Greek culture that was later to affect the Romans so profoundly. The Augustan poet Virgil enshrined the Roman ideal in the **Aeneid**, when Aeneas, legendary Trojan ancestor of the Roman people, descends into the underworld to meet with the spirit of his father, and hear foretold the destiny of his descendants.

'The art of Rome shall be to rule the world, to impose the tradition of peace, to spare the meek and crush the proud'.

So it may be seen that the early Roman was practical and primitive, without the opportunity or incentive to develop the spiritual capacity of the poet, artist and thinker. The decadent society is naturally one that affords its inhabitants sufficient leisure to divert themselves from the essential and the commonplace.

Under the imperial system, however, with administration carried out by the imperial court, the frontiers defended by professional armies, and a vast slave population to perform the many menial duties, leisure was a benefit enjoyed by many, and many also had the wealth to make full use of it. The old Roman character, however, refused to die away, but remained deep in the Roman psyche, becoming manifest in various ways, and creating an element of discomfort admidst all the extravagance and pleasure seeking. Amongst the senatorial classes it rose to complain of un-Roman degeneracy and vice. The Augustan historian Livy made great play of this in his **Ab Urbe Condita** (From the Foundation of the City) calling to account the excesses of the present by comparing them with his stirring but contrived and sparsely researched stories of the virtues of older, simpler times. Other historians followed his example – indeed it must be remembered that Roman historians generally came from the senatorial class, who as we have seen were prone to carry an inbred prejudice against emperors in general (or otherwise from the equestrian class, the 'knights' who were the wealthy middle classes); we must therefore read their works with our critical faculties engaged – and indeed amidst all the crimes and follies that are ascribed to Nero, what seems to cause the most opprobrium is the fact that he was artistic and habitually sang and acted upon the public stage, thereby disgracing his position as ruler of the Roman world. Also the fact that Nero was unwarlike, concluding successful peace treaties and with no great inclination to extend the boundaries of empire, seems to attract as much disapproval as the fact that he killed his mother.

More than this senatorial pride in Rome's martial history, the basic earthiness of the Roman temperament was manifested in the general addiction to the cruelty and violence of the arena – itself a debased remnant of ancient religious rites. Again it was Nero – in spite of his popular image as a depraved and cruel tyrant who delighted in the death and carnage of the gladiatorial combats – who actually attempted to ban the killing of gladiators in the arena, so much did he clearly dislike it (there are grounds for believing that Nero initially had the makings of a liberal emperor but was opposed and frustrated in his attempts at various reforms by reactionary elements in the senate; one cannot help but speculate that the senate was perhaps sometimes its own worst enemy) but was forced to abandon the attempt by the Roman mob, who were indignant at having their bloodthirsty pleasures so emasculated. Whatever Nero's faults – and they were many – he is at least to be commended for his determined if clumsy efforts to raise the level of his subjects' cultural aspirations.

The Italian poet Pietro Cossa wrote truly of Nero that 'His heart is Roman, but his mind is Greek.' Here we are at the root of what so many Romans found objectionable. Though Roman culture was based upon that of Greece, the conquered Greek nation of imperial times was a degenerate shadow of its classical self. The satirist Juvenal writes with fury and indignation of a Rome struck by Greece, and filled with wily Greeks and oily orientals. These people, he complains, drifting into Rome admidst the imported comestibles, win precedence over true-born Romans by their talent for flattery, dishonesty and intrigue; they shamelessly court the wealthy and influential in a fashion no poor Roman can match. They are, he implies, practised in such arts by their history of slavish obedience to despotic kings and foreign conquerors, the past degradations of their race equipping them perfectly to thrive in this new imperial age, against which the proud history of Rome has never armed its own sons. Juvenal, true to human nature, consoles himself with the thought that he is at least morally superior to those more successful than he. It makes him perhaps the most vivid and sympathetic of Roman authors.

Another author whose equally gloomy and embittered, if more subtle, personality has combined with his own sheer brilliance to irrevocably colour, if not dominate, the whole view of posterity upon the period of early empire, is the historian Tacitus, who is the prime exponent of the senatorial faction wreaking its revenge upon the imperial system. At the outset of his *Annals of Imperial Rome*, which survives piecemeal, covering the Julio–Claudian dynasty from the death of Augustus, Tacitus asserts disingenuously that he will write free from animosity or prejudice since, writing decades after the death of Nero, last of the Julio–Claudians, he lacks any personal motive for these. He proceeds to give us a series of masterly character assassinations which are never less than compelling, but often we suspect less than fair. What Tacitus truly gives us is a fictionalized account of the facts – 'faction' is the modern term – offering psychological insights and motivations of which he could not possibly have been certain. But as most writers of fiction will probably admit, the whole process has much to do with the exorcising of personal obsession (although in my experience it has as much to do with the **exercising** of obsession).

Tacitus' own obsession is clear. In his early work, the *Agricola*, a biography of his father-in-law the great general, Tacitus writes of the difficulty of serving with integrity as a state official during the terrible reign of the emperor Domitian – last and most paranoid of the upstart Flavian dynasty. Conscious perhaps of the relatively humble origins of his family, Domitian was relentlessly suspicious and savage towards the senate. Tacitus' own terror and hatred of Domitian is horribly clear to us, and although he survived the reign to live and write under the more enlightened rule of Trajan and Hadrian, he never recovered from it mentally, and it colours his works on the lives of earlier emperors, particularly in his hostile study of Tiberius – a study considered unjust by most modern historians – whom Domitian admired, or at least sympathized with, and with whom he shared certain personality traits; not least a liking for solitude which could only seem strange and profoundly sinister to a people as enormously gregarious as the Romans.

So it may be seen that we are to expect a degree of one-sidedness in the works of many Roman authors, and in a volume which devotes itself to Roman decadence we must further expect an unbalanced view of things by the very nature of the subject. But this should not obscure the very remarkable and enduring achievements of these final custodians of the civilization of the ancient world. It is certainly true that they were in general a materialistic people, not possessing any great spiritual capacity. Their observance of the traditional state religion – the agriculturally based rituals and nature gods of their ancestors – had become largely a matter of mere form by imperial times. Educated people had grown too cynical and sophisticated for it. They were superstitious however, and more inclined to favour strange exotic rites – most foreign religions were tolerated in pre-Christian Rome – and addicted to the occult; fortune tellers, astrologers, mystics of all types were popular, in an attempt to fill the spiritual vacuum of the day. They often held pretensions to culture and good taste, yet these were not truly innate Roman qualities, and their love of extravagance and vulgar spectacle must have inspired surreptitious sneers even from the degenerate Greeks of Juvenal's time. Truly creative thought in the spiritual realms of religion and art remained always beyond the reach of most Romans. They must be content to plunder these things from other nations, which was their greatest talent.

Yet it was said of the Greeks conquered by Rome that 'the captives captivated the captors' and it is true that the Romans learned to value and revere the varied treasures of antiquity that their empire inherited. Imperial Rome may have started as a bandits' cave, yet it became a shrine and a symbol as its inhabitants followed their destiny: making roads, cities, defences and laws; creating and administrating an orderly world in which the legacy of civilization might be preserved.

Contrary to what is often believed, the Roman empire did not collapse as a result of moral decay, but as a consequence of internal disunity and military strife, which made it finally vulnerable to the many barbarian enemies on its frontiers. It should be borne in mind that in spite of the grand scale immorality, degeneracy, cruelty, extravagance and vice contained in these pages, the empire not only endured but remained supreme for centuries after. And that when the western empire finally fell in the fifth century, Europe was plunged into a dark age which was to last a thousand years.

Ovid

43 BC–AD 17?

Augustan Poet

Publius Ovidius Naso was the writer of numerous works, largely of an irreverent and erotic nature. He incurred the displeasure of the emperor Augustus, whose attempts at moral reform Ovid's works blatantly flouted. He was finally exiled around AD 8 for obscure reasons (other than Augustus' general disapproval) to Tomi (modern Constanza) in Romania, where he remained in misery until he died, in spite of numerous letters and poems sent to Rome pleading for imperial clemency. The following poem is from 'The Amores'.

OVID

From *The Amores*

III, 3

The girl was beautiful and wasn't short of charms,
(I'd tried to get off with her many, many times),
but as we lay there closely in each other's arms
it went all limp and useless! Worst of all the crimes!
It wasn't lack of wanting it. The girl did, too.
But Weary Willy simply dangled like a worm.
The girl tried everything to help me that she knew:
with snow-white arms she clasped and held me firm,
she used her tongue a lot when she was kissing me,
and pressed her luscious thighs against me good and quick,
and said things, fed my male machismo-fantasy,
and used the words that usually do the trick.
But still my tool hung slack and flaccid, in a state
too lazy for the amorous plans that I had made.
I lay there like a useless tree-trunk, sheer dead weight,
maybe a corpse, or maybe like some ghostly shade.
What will old age be like (if I should live so long),
if right now, while I'm in my youthful prime, I fail
to score? It shames me to be male and young and strong.
For all *she* felt, I wasn't strong or young or male.

Like some princess who goes to tend the sacred flame,
she upped and left my bed, just as a sister might.
I'd managed twice with Hilda, thrice with What's-Her-
Name,
when with them I performed with vigour and with
might!
And then there was Corinna! *Much* more of the same.
I think we did it nine times in a single night.

Maybe some rot-gut Grecian wine had spiked my sex

and left me drooping? Or maybe some herb or charm
had hurt me, or a witch transfixed me with her hex,
or stuck pins in a waxen me, to cause my liver harm?
They say a spell can lay a wheatfield waste and bare,
and also that a charm can make a well run dry,
cause grapes to fall off vines, from oak-trees acorns tear,
and leave the fruit-trees barren. If it's true, then why
should some magician not have made me slack and slow –
his potion maybe left me lying limply there?
Shame played its part as well – shame dealt me such a blow
that it became a second reason for despair.

When did I ever see or touch a girl like her?
(and like a figure-hugging dress to me she'd clung!)
To touch her would have stirred the Ancient Mariner,
or livened up Methuselah and made *him* young.
And she was mine to touch – but with my hands, and not
my manhood! Gods, what can I pray for from today?
I bet the gods regret they gave me such a lot
of gifts, since seemingly I just threw them away!
Each single thing that I desired was given me:
a welcome, kisses (lots!), alone with her (oh yes!)
Good luck? It's use, not ownership that counts. Only
a miser could just gloat at, not use such *richesses*.
Like Tantalus, imprisoned in the roaring flood,
I eyed the fruit that I could never ever taste.
Nobody leaves a woman's bed at dawn, fit to
go straight to church, all sanctified and pure and chaste.

Oh, when I think of all those fine seductive tricks
she tried – those splendid kisses, too, all lost on me!
She could have got a rise out of an oak-tree – bricks,
or even diamonds would have melted easily.
I'm sure she could have loved a lively, lusty man,
but I was listless, not the man I used to be.
And why play music for a man who's deaf? And can
a man get much from paintings if he cannot see?
How many different variations on the game

did I not try and conjure up inside my head!
But still John Thomas dangled lifeless just the same,
much limper than a rose cut yesterday, half-dead –

and NOW! Just look how stiff and firm it's sticking out,
all eager for the job and spoiling for the fight!
You wretched organ! Down! The shame you've brought
about!
You've tricked me with such promises before tonight!
It's you! It's you who left me weaponless, unmanned,
up to my neck in it, in shame and misery!
My girl left nothing out; she even tried her hand
at massaging some movement into old John T.
But none of her great skills could make it raise its head
and so, alas, she had to watch it droop and fall,
and then 'What's this? What *are* you playing at?' she said,
'who let your droopy limbs into my bed at all?
Either the Wicked Witch has spooked you with something,
or else you've come here straight from someone else's bed!'
No more ado! She left, her nightgown fluttering,
and showed a lovely flash of bare feet as she fled.

But lest her serving-women guessed there'd been no act,
she splashed about some water, to conceal the fact.

Suetonius

Born AD 69/70

Imperial Biographer

Gaius Suetonius Tranquillus held a number of offices involving imperial records and correspondence at the court of the emperor Hadrian, until he was eventually dismissed for some affront given to the empress Sabina. It is to the inestimable benefit of historians that he did not waste the opportunity for research amongst the imperial archives that his position afforded him. His surviving book 'The Twelve Caesars' is an invaluable series of biographies from Julius Caesar to Domitian. He takes particular delight in recounting all manner of salacious gossip. If Tacitus is the greatest of Roman historians, then Suetonius is certainly the most entertaining.

This brief extract from the life of Tiberius describes that emperor's secluded existence in old age upon the Island of Capri. It is probably untrue, the retreat of eminent people from the public gaze always then, as now, likely to give rise to the most outlandish fabrications, but it nevertheless makes fascinating reading.

SUETONIUS

from *The Twelve Caesars*

Tiberius, 43f.

When he retired to Capri, Tiberius planned a private den of vice for himself, a place of forbidden pleasures, in which a huge collection (gathered from all over the place) of girls and of really lecherous men, skilled in unusual practices, would perform sexual acts three-at-a-time – he called them his 'sex-groupies' – so that the sight of them might excite his own flagging passions. Bedrooms on all sides were furnished with highly erotic pictures and statues, and were provided with pornographic books from Elephantis in Egypt, in case anyone missed the point about what they were supposed to do. In the woods and clearings all over the island he had Groves of Lust, where little boys and girls, dressed as Pan or as nymphs stood in front of caves or grottoes, so that the island was now openly and commonly called the 'Caprineum' – 'the home of the randy old goat.'

In fact, his wickedness was even more flagrant – so much so, that one can scarcely allude to it, let alone believe it! He trained young boys – whom he called his 'little fishes' – to swim between his legs and lick him and nibble him to get him going. And he let babies who hadn't yet been weaned suck his genitals like a teat – he had become such a horny old devil! There was a painting by Parrasius (in which Atalanta was giving Meleager a blow-job), which had been left to him on the condition that if he didn't like the subject matter he could have ten thousand sesterces instead. Not only did he prefer it, but he put it up in his bedroom. They do say that while sacrificing once, one of the altar-boys (who had waved the incense) took his fancy. He could hardly wait for the service to end before rushing him (and also his brother, who had sounded the ritual trumpet) outside and ravishing the pair of them. When they complained about this wicked assault, he had their legs broken.

Tiberius, 62

The place of execution is still shown at Capri where the condemned were thrown head-first into the sea after a long and exquisite torture. A band of sailors waited for them below and smashed the bodies with pikes and oars, in case any life remained in them. He thought up this one, among other forms of torture – he'd trick men into getting loaded by drinking large quantities of strong wine, whereupon he would suddenly tie up their private parts so that they would be tortured simultaneously by the tightness of the twine and by the urine. If death had not stopped him, and if Thrasyllus* (deliberately, it is said) had not, through the hope of a longer life, got him to put off certain acts, then very probably many more would have been killed, and he would not even have spared his surviving younger relatives. For he had his suspicions of Gaius Caligula, and he detested Tiberius as a child born of adultery. This is the absolute truth – he used to call King Priam of Troy happy 'because he outlived all of his relations.'

* Tiberius' astrologer.

Suetonius

Life of Caligula

Gaius Caligula, grand-nephew and successor to Tiberius, is one of the most notorious figures in history. He was the youngest of the sons of the hero Germanicus, whose premature death in Antioch plunged the Roman world into grief. Following this his mother and two brothers were imprisoned and executed by Tiberius, whose suspicions against them were inflamed by Sejanus, Tiberius' corrupt and ambitious Guards commander. Sejanus himself was finally revealed to be plotting against Tiberius, and was executed before he moved to destroy Caligula. After this fearful and turbulent early life, Caligula became emperor with all the love and sympathy of the Roman people, who hailed his accession as the dawn of a golden age. His true character, however, irrevocably tainted by his upbringing, soon revealed itself with the acquisition of absolute power.

The translation is an abridged version of the first English translation by Philemon Holland in 1606, revised by Steve Gove.

GAIUS CAESAR CALIGULA

Gaius Caesar was born on the day next preceding the kalends of September, when his father and Gaius Fonteius Capito were consuls. The place of his nativity, by the disagreement of writers, remains uncertain. I myself find among the records, that Antium was the place of his birth.

He got his surname Caligula by occasion of a jest which arose in the camp, because he was brought up there in the habit of an ordinary and common soldier among the rest. Most of all was it shown how far he was able to bear with them through their love and favour by means of his upbringing alongside them, when after the death of Augustus, he alone, through his very sight and presence, quieted them when they were in an uproar and at the very point of furious outrage. For they would not cease to mutiny, until they perceived that he was about to be sent away for danger of the sedition and appointed to the next city adjoining. Then and not before, turning to repentance, they held back his coach, and so by prayer averted the displeasure that was toward them.

He accompanied his father also in the expedition into Syria; from whence being returned, he abode first with his mother, and after she was banished and sent away, he remained with his great-grandmother Livia Augusta; she whom, deceased, he praised in a funeral oration at the Rostra, when he was as yet but a very youth; and then he removed to his grandmother Antonia. From her, in his twentieth year, he was sent for by Tiberius, and upon the same day he did put on his virile gown and withal cut the first down of his beard, without any solemn ceremony, such as his brothers before him had at their coming of age. Here, notwithstanding he was tempted by all the deceitful schemes that those men seeking to draw and force him to quarrels could devise, yet never gave he any opportunity to them, having quite erased from his memory the fall and calamity of his mother, brothers and near friends, as if nothing had befallen to any of them; passing over all those abuses which he had himself endured with incredible dissimulation, being in addition so obedient and dutiful in the service of his grandfather and those about him, that of him it was said and not without good cause: 'A better servant and a worse master there never was.'

Howbeit, his own cruel disposition and villainous nature he could not even then bridle and hold in, but was most willing to be present at all castigations and punishments of those delivered over to execution; and also would he haunt taverns and brothel-houses, and the company of women suspected of adultery, going about from place to place disguised under a wig of false hair, and in a woman's garment; indeed, and most studiously gave his mind to learn the artificial feat of dancing and singing upon the stage. And Tiberius was well content to turn his gaze away and to suffer all these things, if perhaps thereby his fierce and savage nature might have been mollified and become tractable. Which the old man had foreseen well enough long before, insomuch as many times he gave out and said openly, that Gaius lived to the destruction of him and them all; likewise, that he cherished and brought up a very serpent for the people of Rome, and another Phaethon to the whole world.

Not long after he took to wife Junia Claudilla, the daughter of Marcus Silanus, a most noble gentleman. And then he was nominated to succeed as augur in the place of his brother Drusus, and before his investiture therein was advanced to the dignity of priest, a noble testimony of his piety and promise; since, the royal line and imperial court being barren of all other candidates, Sejanus also being suspected and soon afterward overthrown, he should thus by small degrees arise to the hope of succession in the empire. This hope to confirm, after his wife Junia was dead in childbirth, he solicited into filthy wantonness Ennia, the wife of Naevius Macro, then captain of the guard and praetorian cohorts, having also promised her marriage, if he ever attained to the empire; and for assurance hereof he bound his promise with an oath and a letter written by his own hand. Once insinuated by her means into the inward acquaintance of Macro, he attempted the life of Tiberius with poison, as some believe; and whilst he was still living, but labouring for life, commanded his ring to be plucked from his finger – but perceiving that Tiberius attempted to hold fast to it, he forced a pillow over his mouth, and so stifled and strangled him with his own hands; and when his servant made an outcry at this cruel and horrible act, he immediately ordered him to be crucified. And certainly this has the sound of truth, since some authors write that he himself afterwards professed, if not the deed of murder, at least his intention one day to do it. For he made his boast continually, in reporting his own piety, that to avenge the death of his mother and brothers he entered Tiberius' bedchamber with a dagger whilst he lay asleep; and yet from pity thought a second time, flung the weapon from him and went away again. Nor did Tiberius, although he had intelligence of his intent, dare make any inquisition of the matter or proceed to revenge.

Thus having obtained the empire, he gave to the people of Rome, or indeed to all mankind, their hearts' desire; being of all princes that ever were the most wished for by the peoples of the provinces and by the soldiers, because most of them had known him as a child; and favoured by all the people of Rome, in remembrance of his father Germanicus and in compassion for that ruined and extinct household. Therefore as he went from Misenum, albeit he was clad in mourning weeds and reverently attended the body of Tiberius, he was accompanied among the altars, the sacrifices and the burning torches by a great and joyful throng, who besides other lucky and fortunate names called him their star, their chick, their babe, and their nursling.

No sooner was he entered into the city of Rome than immediately the senate and the multitude in the Curia had annulled the will of Tiberius, who in his testament had adjoined unto Gaius as his heir another of his nephews under age; and he was permitted alone to have full and absolute power; and at that there was such universal joy, that before three months had expired, there were according to report above 160,000 beasts slain for sacrifice.

After this, when within some few days he passed over by water but to the nearest islands of Campania, vows were made for his safe return; and there was no man who did let slip the least occasion offered, to testify what pensive care he took as touching his health and safety. And so soon as he had once fallen sick, they all kept watch at night about the palace; and there was no want of men vowing to fight to the last for his life as he lay sick, and indeed devoting their very lives to him if he recovered, professing no less in written bills set up in public places. To this surpassing love of his own citizens and countrymen was adjoined the notable favour also of foreign states. For Artabanus, king of the Parthians, professing always his hatred and contempt of Tiberius, sought of his own accord to Gaius for peace and friendship: indeed, he came in person to a conference with one of his legates who had been consul, and, passing over Euphrates, paid homage to the eagles and other military ensigns of the Romans, and likewise the images of the Caesars.

He also enkindled and set more on fire the affections of men with all manner of acts. When he had with many tears praised Tiberius in funeral oration before the body of the people, and performed most honourably his obsequies, he hastened at once to Pandataria and Pontiae, in foul and tempestuous weather, to bring from thence the ashes of his mother and brother, so that his piety and kindness might the more be seen. And having come to their relics, he very devoutly bestowed them in pitchers with his own hands. And with no less show of pageantry, he sailed with them first to Ostia, with streamers pitched fore and aft in a galley guided by two ranks of oars, and thence to Rome up the Tiber; and accompanied by the most worshipful gentlemen of Rome he conveyed them within two frames devised for the purpose into the mausoleum at noon-day, when the greatest number of people were assembled there. Likewise, in memorial of them he ordained yearly dirges and sacrifices to be performed with pious devotion to their spirits by the whole city. And more, he instituted in honour of his mother solemn games within the circus and also a sacred chariot, in which her image, made to her full living size, should be carried in ceremony. But in remembrance of his father he called the month September Germanicus.

These ceremonial duties done, by virtue of one sole act of the senate, he heaped upon his grandmother Antonia the sum of those honours Livia Augusta had received in her whole time. His uncle Claudius, a knight of Rome until that time and no better, he took to be his colleague in the consulship. His brother Tiberius he adopted the very day that he put on his virile gown, and styled him prince of the youth. As touching his sisters, he caused in all oaths this clause to be annexed: 'Neither shall I prize myself more dear than I do Gaius and his sisters.' In the same way, he ordained that, in the moving and propounding of matters by the consuls to the senators, they should begin in this form: 'That which may be to the good and happy estate of Gaius Caesar and his sisters.' In the similar vein of popularity, he restored all who had been condemned, confined, and exiled, indeed he let them all go free, pardoning whatever crimes or accusations still remained from aforetime. So that no informer or witness should afterwards need to fear, he brought together into the forum all the books and registers pertaining to the causes of his mother and brothers; where, making declaration to the gods that he had neither read nor in any way tampered with them, he burned them. A certain pamphlet presented unto him concerning his life and safety he would not receive, but stood firm that he had done nothing for any person to bear malice towards him; and saying that he had no ears open for informers and tale-bearers.

He expelled forth from Rome the *spintriae*, inventors of monstrous forms in perpetrating filthy lust, being hardly and with much ado entreated not to drown them in the deep sea. The writings of Titus Labienus, Cordus Cremutius, and Cassius Severus, which had been called in and abolished by divers acts of the senate, he suffered to be sought out again, to be in the possession of men and generally to be read, seeing that it stood above all to his duty, to have all actions and deeds delivered to posterity. The history of the empire he published, which by Augustus had been begun diligently, but which was discontinued by Tiberius. To the magistrates he granted free jurisdiction and that there might be no appealing to himself. The gentry and knighthood of Rome he reviewed with severity and great preciseness, yet not without some moderation of his hand. From those in whom was found any foul reproach or ignominy, he openly took their horses; as for those who were culpable in smaller matters, he only passed over their names in reading the roll. To the end that the judges might be eased of their labour, to the four former seats of judgement he added a fifth. He attempted likewise to establish again the ancient manner of elections and to restore to the people their free voices.

The legacies due by the last will and testament of Tiberius (although it was abolished), and also that of Livia Augusta, which Tiberius had suppressed, he caused faithfully and without fraud to be tendered and fully paid. The tax upon all bargains and sales he remitted throughout Italy. The losses that many a man had sustained by fire he supplied; and to those princes whose kingdoms he restored, he adjoined also the fruit and profits of their rents, customs and imposts growing to the Crown in the time between; as to one Antiochus Commagenus who had been confiscate and fined a hundred million sesterces. And that he might the more be considered a favourer of all good examples, he gave to a woman, by nature a libertine, 800,000 sesterces, because she concealed under the most grievous tortures, and would not reveal on pain of death, a wicked act committed by her patron. For such acts, among other honours done him, it was decreed that upon a certain day every year a shield of gold should be brought for him into the Capitol by the colleges of the priests, and that they be accompanied by the senate, and by the children of the nobles both boys and girls, who should sing the praises of his virtues in sweetly tuned verses. Moreover a decree was passed, that the day on which his rule began should be called Parilia, implying thereby as it were a second foundation of the city.

He bore four consulships: the first, from the kalends of July for two months; the second, from the kalends of January, for thirty days; the third, until the ides of January; and the fourth, until the seventh day before the said ides. Of all these, he held the last two jointly together; the third he alone entered upon at Lugdunum, not, as some believe, from pride or negligence, but because, being absent, he could not know that his colleague had died upon the very day of the kalends. He twice gave a gift to the people of three hundred sesterces apiece, and so often a most bounteous dinner for the senate and the nobles, and also for their wives and children. In the latter of these dinners he gave in addition to the men, garments to be worn on public occasions; to the women and children he gave precious trimmings for their robes, of purple and violet colour. And that he might augment the public joy of the city in perpetuity, he added to the feast of Saturnalia one day more, and named it Juvenalis.

He set forth games of sword-fencers, partly in the amphitheatre of Taurus, and partly within the Septa in Mars Field. Into these he brought the very best troops of African and Campanian fighters to do battle by companies. Nor was he always himself president at these solemnities and public shows, but on occasions enjoined the magistrates or else his friends, to take charge of the presidency. As for stage-plays, he exhibited them continually in divers places and in sundry sorts, once even at night-time, burning lights throughout the city. Likewise he cast and scattered among the common people gifts of many kinds to scramble for, and gave out, to each man, panniers with foodstuffs therein. At which feasting he gave to a gentleman of Rome standing next to him and feeding himself most heartily with a greedy stomach, his own share; as also he sent for the same reason to a senator letters patent, thereby declaring him praetor in the most exceptional fashion. He arranged also many circus-games, offering at one while the baiting of panthers, another while jousting and tournaments. But there were some special sports above the rest, when the arena was laid with vermilion, and none but men of senator's rank drove the chariots. Some games he staged upon a whim, namely those called for by spectators in neighbouring galleries when he looked out to observe the preparation of the arena.

Furthermore he devised a new kind of spectacle, such as was never heard of before. For over the three miles' space between Baiae and the dams at Puteoli he made a bridge, having gathered together cargo ships from all parts and placed them at anchor in a double row with a bank of earth cast upon them, direct and straight in the fashion of the Appian highway. He went to and fro upon this bridge for two days; the first day he was mounted on a richly trapped steed and appeared most brave and handsome in a chaplet of oak branches, armed with a battle-axe, a light shield and a sword, and clad in a cloak of gold; the day after he came forth in the garb of a charioteer, riding in a chariot drawn by two fine horses of excellent pedigree, carrying before him Dareus a boy, one of the Parthian hostages, with a train of the praetorian soldiers marching behind in battle array, and accompanied by the cohort of his minions in British wagons. Most men are of the opinion that Gaius invented such a bridge in emulation of Xerxes, who to the wonder of the world made a bridge of planks over the Hellespont, an arm of the sea somewhat narrower than this; others believe that by the rumour of some huge and monstrous piece of work, he might terrify Germany and Britain, upon which countries he meant to make war. But I remember well that, being a boy, I heard my grandfather report the cause of this work as it had been told by his courtiers; namely that the great astrologer Thrasyllus had assured Tiberius, when he was troubled in mind about his successor, that Gaius should no more become emperor than be able to pass to and fro on horseback over the gulf of Baiae.

He set forth shows even in foreign parts, to wit, in Sicily at Syracuse, the games called Actiaci; and at Lugdunum in Gaul, plays of various kind and subject, and also a solemn contest for the prize in eloquence both in Greek and Latin. It is said that in this trial, those who were overcome conferred rewards upon the winners, and were indeed forced to make compositions in their praise. But the worst were commanded to wipe out their own writings, either with a sponge or else with their tongues, unless they wished to be chastised with sticks or else to be ducked over their heads in the nearest river.

The buildings left half-undone by Tiberius, namely the temple of Augustus and the theatre of Pompey, he finished. He began moreover a canal in the Tiburtine territory, and an amphitheatre near to the enclosure called Septa: of the two works the one was completed by his successor Claudius, the other was quite abandoned. He re-fortified the walls at Syracuse, which by the injury of time were decayed and fallen down, and repaired the temples of the gods there. He fully purposed too to rebuild the palace of Polycrates at Samos, to finish the temple of Apollo at Miletus, and also to found and build a city upon the top of the Alps; but, above all, to dig through the isthmus in Achaia: to this end he had already sent to take measure of the work, one who had been captain of a leading cohort, and who was a man of great purpose.

Thus far we have told of a prince; now must we relate as of a monster. Having taken upon himself many surnames, for he was called 'kind', 'the son of the camp', 'father of hosts', and 'the most gracious and mighty Caesar', he happened to hear certain kings, who had come to the city to do their duties and to pay him honour, contend, as they sat with him at supper, about the nobility of their birth and parentage. Of a sudden he cried forth:

One Sovereign Lord, one King let there be,

and almost at once had he taken to himself the diadem and wholly converted the display of empire into the form of a kingdom. But being told that he was exalted already above the state both of emperors and kings, from that time he began to assume to himself a divine majesty; and having given order that the most splendid images of the gods, both those to which the most devout worship was offered, and those which exhibited the finest and most ornate workmanship (among which was that of Jupiter Olympius), should be brought from Greece to Rome, he had their heads removed and his own likeness set in their place. He enlarged the Palace as far as the Forum; likewise changing the temple of Castor and Pollux into a kind of porch, he would stand between the two brother gods as an object for the adoration of all comers. And there were some who saluted him by the name of Jupiter Latiaris.

Moreover he ordained a temple to his own godhead, and along with it priests and the most exquisite offerings. In his temple stood his own image all of gold, to his full height and most lifelike, and dressed each day in clothing as he himself wore. The masterships of his priesthood were purchased at their vacancy by the richest men, those who made greatest suit and offered most therefor. The aforesaid offerings were of flamingoes, peacocks, woodcocks, pheasants and divers other fowls, and these were to be sorted by their kinds, and so every day killed. And truly, he would of custom at night call to the moon, when she was shining full and most brightly, to come and lie with him in his arms; but in the daytime he talked secretly and apart with Jupiter Capitolinus, sometimes whispering to him in the ear, at others speaking out loud and on occasion harshly; for he was heard to utter in threat these words: 'I will remove and banish thee to the land of the Greeks,' until (this was his own telling of the tale), being invited by

Jupiter himself to live with him, he built a bridge over the sacred temple of Augustus, so joining together the Palace and the Capitol. And soon afterward, so that he might be nearer to him, Gaius laid the foundation of a new house in the empty lower court of the Capitol.

He could in no wise abide to be named nephew of Agrippa by reason of his lowly parentage; indeed, he would be angry if any man, either in oration or verse, inserted his name among those of the Caesars. But he gave it out openly, that his own mother was begotten by incest which Augustus committed with his own daughter Julia. And not content with this infamous imputation of Augustus, he straitly forbade his Actian and Sicilian victories to be celebrated yearly with solemn holidays, as being unlucky and hurtful to the people of Rome. As for Livia Augusta his great-grandmother, he called her time and again Ulysses in a woman's habit; indeed, in a certain epistle to the senate he was so bold as to assert her ignobility, that she was descended from a decurion who was her grandsire on the mother's side, whereas it is plain according to the public records that her grandfather Aufidius Lingo held honourable offices in Rome. When his grandmother Antonia requested secret conference with him, he refused her unless Macro, captain of the guard, might be also present to hear their talk. And so by such indignities as these he was the cause of her death; and yet, as some think, he gave her poison also. Nor allowed he any honour to her when she was dead, but beheld the burning of her funeral pyre from his dining-chamber.

His brother Tiberius he surprised unawares, sending a tribune of soldiers who rushed in upon him and so slew him. Likewise he forced Silanus, his father-in-law, to death by cutting his own throat with a razor, picking quarrels with them both upon these causes: that the one would not follow him when he voyaged upon a sea much troubled and very rough, but stayed behind in hope to seize the city of Rome for himself, if by occasion of tempests the voyage should go awry; the other smelled strongly of a preservative or antidote, as if he had taken the same against Gaius' poisons. Yet in truth, Silanus thus avoided the insufferable pain of seasickness and the harsh discomforts of sailing; and Tiberius but took medicine for a continual cough which grew worse day by day. As for his uncle Claudius, Gaius bore him in so low regard as to make of him a mere figure of fun and a laughing-stock.

His sisters he would dishonour as of daily custom; at any great feast he would place one or other of them by turns beneath himself at table, while his wife sat above. Of these sisters (as it is believed to be true), he deflowered Drusilla being a virgin, when he himself was yet under age and a very boy; and one time above the rest he was found in bed with her and taken in the manner by his grandmother Antonia, in whose house they were brought up both together. And afterwards, when Drusilla had been given in marriage to Lucius Cassius Longinus, a man of consular degree, he took her from him and kept her openly, as if she had been his own lawful wife. Also when he lay sick, he ordained her to be heir of all his goods and furthermore to succeed him in the empire. For the same sister deceased he proclaimed a general cessation of the law, during which time it was a capital crime for any man to laugh, or bathe, or sup together with parents, wife or children. And having wearied of his sorrow, he fled suddenly out of the city by night, and passed all throughout Campania, and thence to Syracuse; and returned again speedily with his beard and hair of head overgrown. Nor at any time after, in making a speech before the people or to his soldiers, even in the gravest of matters, would he swear otherwise than by the name of Drusilla. His other sisters, Livia and Agrippina, he loved neither with such tender affection nor so good respect, but many times prostituted and offered them to be abused by his own stale catamites. And in such wise he condemned them the more readily in the case of Aemilius Lepidus, as adulteresses and privy to the plots and treasons addressed against his person. And he not only uncovered by guile and adulteries the source of writings against him, but also consecrated to Mars Revenger the three daggers prepared by the conspirators for his death, with an inscription over them containing the cause of his so doing.

As for his marriages, a man may scarcely discern whether he contracted, dissolved, or held them with more dishonesty. He commanded to be brought home to him as his own wife Livia Orestilla, while she was wedded to Gaius Piso, having himself been present at the solemnisation of the marriage; and having but a few days later cast her from him, after two years he banished her, because she was thought in the time between to have had again the company of her former husband. Some report that, being an invited guest at the nuptial supper, he commanded Piso in these terms: 'Sir, see you sit not too close to my wife', and upon this had her away with him from the table; and the next day published a proclamation that he had made a marriage after the example of Romulus and Augustus. As regarding Lollia Paulina, married already to Gaius Memmius, a man of consular degree and ruler of armies, upon mention of her grandmother as the most beautiful lady in her time, he all of a sudden commanded her return from the province and, taking her from her husband, wedded her and soon turned her away, forbidding her straitly for ever the use of any man's body whatsoever.

Caesonia he loved with more ardent affection and constancy; not for any special beauty and favour of her own above others, nor yet because she was in the flower of her youth (she had been the mother already of three daughters by another man), but only because she was a most lascivious woman and of insatiable lust; his regard for her being such that he would display her to his soldiers clad in a soldier's tunic with shield and helmet, riding next to him; but he showed her to his friends stark-naked also. Only when she brought him a child, did he vouchsafe her the title of wife, and not before; and he made it known abroad, that in a single day he was become both her husband and also father of the infant born of her body. This child he named Julia Drusilla, and he carried her about through all the temples of the goddesses, bestowing her at last in the lap of Minerva, and commending the place to her for her nourishment, upbringing and education. And there was no surer sign to show that she was his own and conceived of his own seed than her curstness and shrewdness; and wicked was she from the first, in such measure that with her cruel fingers she would not stick to lay at the faces and eyes of other small children playing together with her.

Vanity it would be and mere folly to add, how he served his kinsfolk and friends, to wit Ptolemy, King Juba's son and his own first cousin, but especially Macro himself, and likewise Ennia, who were his chief helpers and advanced him to the empire. All of them, by right of their near relation and in consideration of their good deserts, were most highly rewarded with bloody death. Nor was he one whit more respectful of the senate, nor did he deal more gently with them; some, after they had borne the highest honours, he made to run beside his wagon in their gowns for many miles, or to stand in wait for him at supper girt about with a white linen towel, now at the head of the table, now at the foot. Others, whom he had had secretly murdered, he continued nevertheless calling for as if they were yet alive, giving it out most untruly some few days after, that they had wilfully made themselves away. The consuls once had forgotten by chance to publish by proclamation his birthday, for which he deprived them of their magistracy; and so for three days the commonwealth was without the sovereign authority. His own quaestor, who happened to be nominated in a conspiracy against him, he caused to be scourged, and had the clothes stripped from him put under the soldiers' feet, that they might stand more steadily while whipping him.

With equal pride and violence he dealt with other states and degrees of citizens. Being disturbed by the commotion of those who took their places in the circus by midnight (for which they had to pay nothing), he drove them all away with cudgels; in which tumult and hurly-burly there were above twenty knights of Rome crushed to death, and as many of their wives, besides an infinite number of the common multitude. At the stage-plays, being minded to sow discord and minister occasion of quarrel between the commons and gentlemen of Rome, he had the finest and most prominent places filled early, even by the basest commoners who came. At the sword-fight, he would give command that the shades be folded up during the most parching heat of the sun, and forbade that any person should be let forth; and then, removing and sending quite away the ordinary furniture of shows, he put before the people poor wild beasts and carrion-lean to be baited, and, to do combat, the sword-fencers most lowly and worn with age, and he sent out to carry them well-known citizens and men of quality, but such as were noted for some special feebleness and imperfection of body. And at many other times he brought dearth and famine among the people, by shutting up the garners and storehouses from them.

By these examples he showed the cruelty of his nature most of all. When cattle, those used to feed wild beasts prepared for baiting, grew in price very dear, he had criminals who had been found guilty slaughtered for the purpose. And in reviewing the jails and the prisoners therein he, taking no account of the cause of their imprisonment, commanded all, sparing no man's head, to be led forth to execution. From a man who had sworn to perform his duty in public sword-fight for the recovery of Gaius' health, he exacted the performance of the vow, and watched him fighting at sword-point; nor would he dismiss him until he was victor. And there was another who for the same cause had vowed to die. This man, not being very forward to pay his vow, he had adorned with sacred herbs and decorations, like a sacrifice; and he was delivered into the hands of boys who, calling upon him to discharge his vow, were to drive him through the streets of the city, until he was thrown headlong down the steep ramparts. Many honest citizens of good estate, after he had first disfigured them with marks of branding irons, he condemned to dig in mines, to build highways, or to fight with beasts; or he kept them on all fours like brute creatures in a cage, or else slit them through the midst with a saw. And those whom he thus treated were not all of them guilty of any grievous offences; it was sufficient that they might have spoken meanly of some show that he exhibited, or that they had not sworn stoutly by his genius.

He forced parents to be present at the execution of their own children. And when one father excused himself by reason of sickness, he sent a litter for him; another, immediately after the heavy spectacle of his own son put to death, Gaius invited to his own table, made him great cheer, and by all manner of courtesy provoked him to jocoseness and mirth. The master of his sword-fights and beast-baitings he had for many days beaten with chains in his own sight; and had near killed him, before he could no longer abide the stench of his brain by this time putrefied. A poet for a verse that he made, implying a jest which might be doubly taken, he burnt at the stake in the very middle showplace of the amphitheatre. A gentleman of Rome whom he had cast before wild beasts, he commanded to be brought back, after he cried out that he was innocent; and after he had cut out his tongue, sent him back among them, to fight for his life or else to be devoured.

Having recalled from exile a man who had been long banished, he demanded of him what he was wont to do in his place of banishment; the man replied thus by way of flattery, 'I prayed without cease to the gods that Tiberius, as has now come to pass, might perish, and you become emperor.' Hereupon Caligula, believing that those whom he had banished prayed likewise for his death, sent into the islands to have them killed every one. Being desirous to have a certain senator mangled and torn to pieces, he persuaded other men, that they should of a sudden, as this said senator entered the Curia, call him enemy to the State, and violently seize him; and when with their writing-irons they had stabbed him all over, they were to deliver him to the rest, to be dismembered and cut in pieces.

Neither was he satisfied until he saw the man's limbs, joints and innards drawn along the streets, and piled together all in a heap before him.

His deeds, most horrible as they were, he augmented with as cruel words. He used to say that he commended and approved in his own nature nothing more than immovable rigour. When his grandmother Antonia seemed to admonish him, he said to her (as though it were not enough to disobey her), 'Go to, old woman, remember I may do what I will against all persons whomsoever.' Being minded to kill his own brother, whom he imagined for fear of poison to have fortified himself with preservatives, 'What!' quoth he, 'is there any antidote against Caesar?' When he had banished his sisters, he threatened them in these terms, saying that he had not only islands at his command, but swords also. A certain citizen of praetor's rank sought often, from his place of retirement at Anticyra (to which isle he would go for his health's sake), to have his office renewed. But instead he gave order that the man should be killed outright, adding these words, that bloodletting was necessary for him, who had gained no good from hellebore. Every ten days his practice was to note and write down the names of a certain number from the jail for execution, saying that thereby he reckoned up and cleared his book of accounts. When he had at one time condemned a host both of Gauls and Greeks together, he made his boast that he had subdued Gallograecia.

He would not permit any to die until they had received many strokes, making this precept which became well-known and notorious: 'Strike so as they may feel they are dying.' He executed on one occasion a man whom he had not appointed to die, merely by error and mistaking his name: 'But it makes no matter,' said he, 'for even he has also deserved death.' This speech of the tyrant from a tragedy he often repeated: 'Let them hate me, for thus they fear me.' Many a time he bitterly accused all the senators at once, that they were the dependants and adherents of the traitor Sejanus, or informers against his mother and

brothers, bringing forth the evidence which before he had
pretended burnt; and so excused and justified the cruelty of
Tiberius as necessary, seeing that he could not choose but
to believe the intelligence of so many. Those of the rank of
gentlemen he railed at continually, that they were devoted
wholly to the stage and show-place. One time, being
highly displeased with the multitude, since they favoured
in fight his man's opponent, he said, 'Would God that the
people of Rome had but one neck.' It once happened that
five swordsmen, fighting both singly and in company, had
yielded without combat to as many other champions or
fencers. Now when command was given by the people
that the vanquished should be killed, one of them took up
his spear again into his hand and slew all the five who were
thought the victors. This slaughter he bewailed in an edict
as most cruel, and also cursed them who endured to see the
sight.

He was wont moreover to complain openly of the time
wherein he lived, as distinguished by no public calamities;
whereas the reign of Augustus was memorable for the
overthrow of Varus, that of Tiberius ennobled by the fall
of the scaffolding in the theatre at Fidenae. As for himself,
he was sure to be forgotten, such was the general well-
being in his days. And always he wished for the destruction
of his armies, for famine, pestilence and raging fires, or for
quakes to rend open the ground.

Even whilst he was at his recreations and pastimes,
whilst he set his mind upon gaming and feasting, he
practised the same cruelty both in word and deed. Often,
as he sat at dinner or banqueted, were serious matters
examined in his sight by means of torture; and a soldier
with the skill and dexterity to behead folk on the very spot
would cut off the heads of prisoners as a matter of course.
At Puteoli, when he dedicated the bridge which, as we
noted before, was his own invention, he invited many of
those present to join him from the shore, then suddenly
turned them all headlong over the bridge into the water.
And seeing some of them taking hold of the rafts to save

themselves, he shoved them off with poles and oars into the sea. At a public feast in Rome, a servant chanced to pluck off a thin plate of silver from the table; and for this he was immediately delivered to the hangman for execution in this wise, that his hands should be cut off and hung about his neck before his breast, and a written title carried before him declaring the cause of his punishment, and he to be so led around all the company as they sat at meat. One of the fencers from the fencing-school once sparred with him, and in the match took a fall, and lay at his feet; him Caligula stabbed with a short iron blade and, in the solemn manner of the victor, paraded up and down with his garland of palms. There was a beast brought to the altar ready to be killed for sacrifice; he came dressed in the habit of beast-slayer, and lifting his axe-head high knocked down the minister himself who was readied to cut the beast's throat, and so dashed his brains out. At a plenteous feast where there was great joy he began all at once to laugh uncontrollably; and when the consuls seated by his side asked gently and with fair language the reason for his laughter, he answered, 'Why, for nothing but that with one nod of my head I can have your throats cut in an instant.'

Among the divers and sundry jests he made, once, as he stood next to the image of Jupiter, he demanded of Apelles, an actor of tragedies, which of the two he thought to be the greater and more stately, Jupiter or himself. And when the player made some delay in his answer, he mangled and tore him with his whip, praising all the time the voice which cried to him for mercy as exceedingly sweet and harmonious, even when the man groaned under his lashes. Each time he kissed the neck of wife or concubine, he would say in the very act, 'As fair and lovely a neck as this is, off it shall go if I but speak the word.' Moreover, he announced many a time, that he would himself fetch out of his wife Caesonia, even with lute-strings, the reason that he loved her so entirely.

Nor did he rage with less envy and malice, pride and

cruelty, against persons from past times and ages. The statues of brave and worthy men, brought by Augustus out of the Capitol courtyard into Mars' Field, he overturned and cast here and there in such fashion that they could not be set up again whole; and he forbade that any statue or image of a living man should be erected, without his granting. He also would have abolished Homer's verses: 'For why may not I,' he said, 'do that which Plato lawfully did, who banished him from the city which he established?' Likewise he went within a little of removing the writings and images of Virgil and Livy both, from all the libraries. The one of these he carped at as a man of no wit and very mean learning; the other for his verbosity and for the careless composition of his history. Moreover, regarding lawyers, as if he meant to take away all use of their skill and knowledge, he announced many times that he would surely bring it to pass, that they might never give any answer but according to plain reason, and should use no eloquence of language.

He took from the noblest families the old arms and badges of their houses; from Torquatus the collar; from Cincinnatus the curled lock of hair; and from Gnaeus Pompeius, from ancient stock descended, the surname of Magnus belonging to his lineage. As for King Ptolemy (of whom I made report before), when he had both sent for him from his own kingdom and also honourably entertained him, he slew him all of a sudden; and this for no reason in the world but that, as he entered the amphitheatre to see the games there exhibited, he perceived Ptolemy had the eyes of all the people upon him with the resplendent brightness of his purple robe. All those who were handsome and had a fine long head of hair, he disfigured by shaving their skulls behind. There was a certain Aesius Proclus, whose father had been a principal captain of the foremost cohort, who for his exceeding tall stature and fine figure was called Colosseros; this man he had pulled down suddenly from where he sat, and had him brought into the arena in the lists, where he was matched in fight first with a lightly-armed fencer, and then with a swordsman fully armoured. Now when he had gained twice the upper hand, he commanded him at once to be seized and bound fast, and being put into foul and tattered clothes to be led around the streets to be displayed to women, and so finally to have his throat cut. To conclude, there was none of so lowly condition, nor of so mean rank, that his better qualities he did not despoil.

It also happened, on a day of public games, that there was greater applause and more clapping of hands than was usual, when Porius the fencer released his slave in admiration for the brave combat he had made. At this, Caligula flung himself out of the theatre in such haste that, treading upon the hem of his gown, he came tumbling down the stairs head over heels, chafing and fuming, and exclaiming that the people of Rome, lords of all nations, gave greater honour, and that on a most vain and frivolous occasion, to a sword-fencer, than they gave to himself there present.

No regard had he of chastity or cleanness, either in himself or in others. Marcus Lepidus, Mnester the panto-mime, and also certain hostages he kept and loved, as the saying went, by way of reciprocal commerce in mutual impurity, in the doing and suffering of unnatural acts. Valerius Catullus, a young gentleman descended from a family of consul's rank, complained and cried out openly that he was unnaturally abused by him, and that his very sides were wearied and tired out with his filthy company. Over and above the incests committed with his own sisters and his notorious love of Pyrallis, that common prostitute and strumpet, there was scarcely a woman of any honour or reputation whom he left unsullied. For the most part he would invite these with their husbands to supper, and as they passed at his feet would peruse them closely and intently at his leisure, as if they were wares bought and sold at market; and he would with his hand chuck them under the chin and make them look up, if any of them held down their faces in modesty and shyness. And then, whenever he desired, he would leave the dining-room, and when he had summoned to him in his private chamber the woman whom he liked best, he would shortly after return, while the signs of his wanton work were yet fresh, and openly either praise or dispraise her before all the company; so reckoning up every good or bad part both of her body and action in that brutish business. To some of these women he sent bills of divorce in the name of their absent husbands, and commanded these to be set upon the file and to stand in public record.

In riotous and wasteful expense he surpassed the schemes and inventions of all the prodigal spendthrifts there ever were, devising new ways and habits of bathing, alongside most strange and monstrous kinds of foodstuffs, for example to bathe himself with ointments both hot and cold, and to set upon the table at feasts before his guests loaves and other dishes all of gold, saying at the same time, that a man must either be frugal or else Caesar. Moreover, for days at a time he cast among the common people from the window of the stately basilica Julia, coins of no mean value. He built, in addition, tall sailing-ships of cedarwood, their poops and sterns set with precious stones, their sails of many colours, and within them baths, great galleries, promenades, and dining-chambers of vast capacity, containing vines and apple-trees and many other fruits; and here he would sit feasting all day among choirs of musicians and melodious singers, and so sail along the coasts of Campania. In the building of stately palaces and manor-houses in the country he cast aside all rules and orders, as though he desired nothing so much as to do what had been thought impossible to be done. And to this end he laid foundations where the sea was most tempestuous and deepest, and hewed rocks of the hardest flint and most jagged; he raised plains level with mountains and, digging down hill-tops, lowered them to the plains; and all this with the greatest urgency, so that he punished those who worked slowly with very death. In sum, and without the reckoning of each item in particular, the vast wealth and mass of treasure which Tiberius Caesar left behind him, valued at 2700 millions of sesterces, he consumed to nothing before the passing of but a single year.

His wealth therefore exhausted and grown to nothing, he turned his mind to the seizure of goods by various and cunning deceptions, by sales and taxes. He levied and gathered new tributes and imposts such as were never heard of before, at first by the hands of the tax-collectors, but afterwards (by reason of the excessive sums thus gained) by the centurions and tribunes of the praetorian cohorts. For he omitted no kind of thing, no manner of person, but imposed some kind of tribute upon them all.

After such taxes were proclaimed, but not yet published abroad in writing, so that through ignorance of the law many transgressions were committed, he finally, upon the demand of the people, published the act; but it was written in such small letter and such an obscure place that no man might copy it out to make it more widely known. And so that there should be no kind of plunder which he did not attempt, he set up a brothel in the very palace itself, with many rooms and chambers furnished according to the dignity and worth of that place; and in it were installed as prostitutes married women and freeborn youths both. Then he sent to all the public places, to markets and meeting-places, to invite and call by name young men and old alike to fulfil and satisfy their lust. All comers at their entrance paid money to be lent again at interest. Certain persons were also appointed to take note in open sight of the names of those who entered, as that they were good friends increasing the revenues of Caesar.

But when on one occasion he had a daughter born to him, complaining then of his poverty and the weight of expense that lay upon him both as emperor and also as a father, he accepted the voluntary contributions and gifts of men toward the provision of the girl's food, and also toward her dowry. He declared also by edict that he would receive New-year's offerings; and so he stood, on the first day of January, in the porch of his house, ready to accept whatever pieces of money came, and the multitude of all ranks poured out with full hands and generous hearts bounty upon him. Finally, he burned so with the desire to handle money, that often he would walk up and down upon heaps of coins, and wallow with his whole body among huge piles of gold pieces, strewn here and everywhere in a great open place.

Of stature he was very tall, pale, and wan-coloured, of body gross and shapeless; his neck and shanks exceedingly slender; his eyes sunk in his head and his temples hollow, his forehead broad, with deep furrows; the hair of his head grew thin, and his crown was all bald; but in all other parts hairy he was and shaggy. It was therefore a heinous and capital offence, to look from a place above upon him as he passed by; or but to speak of a goat on any occasion whatsoever. His face and expression, being naturally stern and grim, he made by purpose more crabbed and hideous, composing it before a looking-glass in all manner of ways so as to seem more terrible and to strike greater fear.

He was neither healthful in body nor sound in mind. Being as a child much troubled with the falling sickness, he was in his youth most careful in bodily exertion, yet still ever and anon, there came upon him a sudden fainting, so that he was scarcely able to walk, to stand, to rise, to recover himself, or even to lift up his head. This infirmity of the mind he well himself perceived, and often would go away to Anticyra, there to purge his brain thoroughly. It is thought, indeed, that he was poisoned with a potion given him by his wife Caesonia, which was yet a love medicine, but one that cracked his wits and enraged him. He was troubled most of all with lack of sleep; for he slept not above three hours in a night, and in those he took no quiet repose, but was filled with the terror of strange illusions and fantastical imaginations; dreaming upon one time that he saw the very form and resemblance of the sea talking with him. And for this reason for most of the night, hour upon hour barely endured as he lay wakeful, one while sitting up in his bed, another roaming and wandering the great expanses of his galleries, he would look out and call for daylight to arrive.

I should not do amiss if to this mind's sickness of his I attributed the vices which in one man were of so contrary a nature, to wit, excessive confidence, and an equal overplus of fearfulness. For he that set so light by the gods and despised them as he did, yet would at the least thunder and lightning shut tight his eyes, wrap and cover his whole head; but if the tumult were great, he would leap from his bed, to creep and hide himself under the bedstead. Then during his travels through Sicily, after he had scorned and made mock of the miraculous and strange sights in many parts of the land, he fled suddenly by night from Messana, with fright at the smoke and rumbling noise of the top of Aetna.

As for his apparel, his shoes and other habit, he wore them neither after the fashion of the country nor of the city, nor as befitting a man; nor even, I may tell you, in the manner of any mortal creature. He would come abroad into the city clad in cloaks of needlework embroidered with divers colours, and set with precious stones; or in a coat with long sleeves, and decked with bracelets. You might see him in his silks, veiled all over in a loose mantle with a train; sometimes going about in Greek slippers, or else in buskins, at other times in a simple pair of brogues or high shoes, such as common soldiers employed in observation used. Now and then was he also seen shod with women's pumps. But for the most part he showed himself abroad with a golden beard, carrying in his hand either a thunderbolt or a three-pronged mace, or else the rod called a caduceus (these being the signs all and the ornaments of the gods), and indeed in the attire and array of Venus. As for his triumphal robes and insignia, he would wear them continually, even before any warlike expedition, and sometimes even the cuirass of Alexander the Great, fetched out of his sepulchre and monument.

Of the liberal arts he gave his mind least to deep literature and sound learning, but most to eloquence, although he was by nature already fair-spoken and of a quick tongue. With no doubt, he had at will both words and sentences with which to plead and declaim against any, were he but once angered. His action, gesture and voice also served him well, insomuch as when, for very heat and earnestness of speech scarcely was he able to stand his ground and keep still in one place, and yet still might no less be heard by them who stood afar off. When he was about to make an oration, his manner was to threaten in these terms, namely that he would draw forth and let drive at his adversary the keen weapon of his night-study; dismissing with contempt the milder kind of writing so far that he said of Seneca, a writer in those days widely favoured, that his compositions were plain exercises for mere show, and that he was no better than sand without lime. His wont was also to answer by writing the orations of those orators who had argued well and to acclaim; too, to meditate and devise accusations and defences of great persons who were impeached in the senate; and having called thither by edict the gentlemen of the city to hear him speak, either to bring low by additional charges, or to ease and give relief to each man by his sentence.

The arts, moreover, and many masteries of different nature, he practised most studiously. A fine sword-fencer he was and charioteer, and yet too a singer and a dancer. He would fight in earnest and with full weaponry, and run a chariot-race in the arenas, which he had built in many places. As for chanting and dancing, so passionate was he that he could not forbear, in the very public theatres and show-places, to join singing with the tragedian as he pronounced, and also openly to copy and imitate the gesture of the player, as it were by way of praise or correction. And truly (as it is thought), on the very day on which he was murdered, he did proclaim a wake or vigil all night long for no other cause than that, by taking the opportunity of the night's licentiousness, he might begin to make his entrance upon the stage. And many times he danced by night; but once above the rest he raised from their beds three honourable persons who had been consuls and sent for them late to the palace; and afraid as they were that some fearful calamity had befallen, he had them raised aloft, and then suddenly, with a great noise of trumpets and sound of horns and cymbals, he came leaping forth in a robe reaching down to his ankles; and after he had danced out the measures to a song, vanished again from their sight. And yet this man, so excellent a scholar as he was in the learning of all other feats, had no skill at all in swimming.

Now those to whom he took a love and a liking, he favoured exceedingly and beyond all reason. Mnester the famous pantomime he had such an affection for, that he did not abash to kiss him even in the open theatre; and if any one, whilst he was dancing or acting a part, made whatsoever little noise in interruption, he commanded that person to be pulled from his place and with his own hand scourged him. A gentleman of Rome chanced to make some stirring whilst the said Mnester was upon the stage; unto him he sent word forthwith by a centurion to depart without delay and go down to Ostia, there to take sea; and he was to carry to King Ptolemy into Mauretania letters, the tenor of which was this: 'To the bearer of these missives, whom I have sent hither to you, see you do neither good nor harm.' Certain of the fencers he made captains over his squires and his bodyguard. A swordsman named Columbus fortuned to wound his favourite and win the victory, but thereby gained he some small hurt; Gaius made no more ado but put poison into the wound, calling it thereupon Columbinum. So devoted was he to the green faction of charioteers that he would take his suppers and make his abode in their quarters. Upon a certain Eutychus, a chariot-driver, he bestowed at a banquet gifts of two millions of sesterces. For the sake of their chariot-steed named Incitatus, he was wont the day before the games in the circus, to send by his soldiers to command the neighbours there adjoining to keep silence, lest the horse be disturbed; and besides he had built for the beast a stable all of marble, and a manger of ivory; over and above this his tackle and harness of purple, with a brooch of precious stones at his bit; and he furnished this stable with servants and household, all to the end that guests invited in his name might be more finely and gaily entertained. It is reported, moreover, that he intended to prefer this very steed to a consulship.

As he thus made riot and carried on outrageously, there were many who lacked neither heart nor will to assault his person. But after one or two conspiracies detected, while other men for lack of opportunity stayed their hands, two at last plotted together and indeed performed their design; and in the knowledge of the highest of his court and the captains of his guard. For even they, being named (though untruly) as privy to a certain conspiracy, perceived themselves suspected and odious to him for that reason. For at once he had them brought to a secret place, and protested with sword drawn that he would die by his own hand, if they also thought him worthy of death. And he did not cease from that time onward, to accuse one privately to another, and to set them one against the other. Now these conspirators resolved to assail him during the Palatine games, as he departed out of the theatre at noontide; and Cassius Chaerea, tribune of the praetorian cohort, took it upon him to play the first part in this action, that very man now advanced far in years, whom Gaius was wont to mock in most opprobrious terms as a wanton and effeminate person, as on such occasion as that when he came to him for a password, he would give him Priapus or Venus, or if at any while he rendered thanks, would gesture to him with his hand, wagging in an obscene and filthy manner.

Many prodigious signs were seen, presaging his future death and murder. The statue of Jupiter at Olympia, which he desired to have broken in pieces and brought to Rome, set up all on a sudden such a mighty laughter that the workmen around it let their engines and vices slip and ran so all away. And at once appeared a man whose name was also Cassius, swearing that he had warning and command in a dream to sacrifice a bull to Jupiter. The Capitol in

Capua on the ides of March was smitten with lightning, and likewise in Rome the porter's lodge belonging to the prince's palace. And there were many to give their conjecture that the one prodigy portended danger to the master of the house from his guard and the attendants of his person; and the other that some notable murder would be done, such as in times past had been committed upon the same day. Also Sulla the astrologer, when Gaius asked him his counsel and opinion concerning the horoscope of his nativity, told him plainly that most certain and inevitable death approached near at hand. In similar wise the oracle at Antium gave him a warning to beware of Cassius; for which very cause he had given order and commandment that Cassius Longinus, then proconsul in Asia, should be killed, not remembering that the foresaid Chaerea was named Cassius.

The day before he lost his life he dreamt that he stood in heaven close to the throne of Jupiter, and that Jupiter spurned him with the great toe of his right foot, and therewith threw him down headlong to the earth. And that same day, each occurrence that happened to him appeared as a prodigy and foretokening of his fall. As he made his sacrifices, he was besprinkled with the blood of the flamingo. And Mnester, the skilful actor abovenamed, presented that very tragedy which once upon a time Neptolemus the tragedian acted at those games wherein Philip, king of the Macedonians, was killed. And when in the show or interlude entitled *Laureolus*, wherein the chief player, making haste to escape the catastrophe, vomited blood, many more of the minor actors strove to attempt the like artifice, and the whole stage was set flowing with blood. There was prepared likewise at night-time another show, wherein the dark tales reported of hell and its infernal spirits were to be exhibited and unfolded by Egyptians and Ethiopians.

Upon the ninth day before the kalends of February, at about one of the clock after noon, wondering to himself whether he should rise to dine or no (for his stomach was still raw and weak from a surfeit of banqueting the day before), at last with the persuasion of friends he went forth. Now, when he met in the cloister with certain boys of noble birth (who had been brought out of Asia to sing hymns and to act out battles upon the stage), who were there preparing themselves, he stood still and stayed there to view and encourage them; and but that the leader of the company said he was very cold, he would have returned and had them perform. But what befell after this is reported in two manner of ways. Some say that, as he spoke to these boys, Chaerea came behind his back, and with the blade of his sword grievously wounded his neck, with the words, 'Mind this'; whereupon Cornelius Sabinus, another of the conspirators, encountered him afront and ran him through in the breast. Others write that Sabinus, after the gathered crowds had been cleared by the centurions (who were privy to the conspiracy), called for a watchword, and when Gaius gave him the word Jupiter, cried out aloud, 'Here take it sure,' and with that Cassius, as Gaius looked behind him, with one slash cut his jaw quite through. Also, as he lay on the ground cowering and cried that he was yet alive, the rest of their accomplices with thirty wounds dispatched and made an end of him. For 'Strike again' was their signal and watchword; and some of them thrust their swords even through his privy members. At the very first noise and outcry, his litter-bearers came running to help with their litter-staves; soon after, the Germans who were his squires came in, and as they slew some of the murderers, so too they killed certain senators who were all innocent.

He lived twenty-nine years and ruled the empire three years, ten months and eight days. His corpse was conveyed secretly to the Lamian orchards where, being but half-burnt in a hastily prepared pyre, it was covered with a few turves of earth cast lightly over it; but afterwards by his sisters now returned from exile, it was taken up, burned to ashes and interred. It is for certain known that before the completion of these solemnities, the keepers of those orchards were troubled by the walking of spirits and ghosts; and in that house wherein he was murdered there passed not a night without some terror or fearful apparation, until the very house itself was consumed by fire. There died together with him both his wife Caesonia, stabbed with a sword by a centurion, and also a daughter of his, whose brains were dashed out against a wall.

What the condition and state was of those days, these particulars will make plain to any man. For when this massacre was divulged and made known abroad, men gave such reporting no credit in the beginning, but there went a suspicion that Gaius himself had feigned and given out a rumour of his murder, by such means to test men's minds and discover how steadfast was their loyalty to him; nor, indeed, had the conspirators destined the empire to anyone, and Rome was headless. And the senators, in recovering their ancient freedoms, agreed that the consuls should be assembled not at the first in the Curia, because it bore the name Julia, but in the Capitol; truly some of them, when their turns came to speak, opined that the memory of the Caesars should be utterly abolished and erased, giving advice that their temples be pulled down. Moreover, it has been especially noted and observed that those of the Caesars, who had the forename of Gaius, beginning with him who was slain in the troublesome days of Cinna, died all of them a violent death.

OVID

III, 14

Since you're so beautiful I cannot ask you to
be faithful, just as long as I (poor wretch!) don't *know*.
I can't command you to be chaste, of course, but do
dissemble, please – try to make sure it doesn't show.

A lady simply hasn't sinned, if sin can be denied.
The only sins that count are those admitted. And in fact
it's mad to broadcast, in broad daylight, far and wide
things done at night-time, yes, or any private act.

An honest whore, about to serve some punter's needs,
will always bolt the door and keep the public out.
So why should you expose to gossip all your deeds,
or spread word of your secret naughtiness about?

Just think a bit! Put on a show of decency,
help me believe (if wrongly) you're a modest child.
Behave as usual, but deny it all for me.
Don't be ashamed to keep your public language mild.

There's one place where a spot of hanky-panky's fine –
enjoy yourself in there! Make sure you get enough!
But when you leave that place, you ought to leave behind
such fun and frolics – that's all strictly bedroom stuff.

In there you can strip off without a shred of shame,
and legs and other legs can lock together tight;
in there French-kissing's just one of the many games
that Venus offers for our manifold delight;
in there there's talking, gasping, naming loving names,
and creaking bedsprings audible all through the night.

But with your frock put on a face of modesty
so that you look too sweet to contemplate the act.
Do it, but tell me otherwise. Don't let me see.
I'd rather stay a fool and keep my faith intact.

Who do I always get to see those billets-doux?
Why do I spot the indentations in your bed,
or see that not just sleep has ruffled your hair-do,
or see the lovebites on your neck when they're still red?
You all but do the job before my very eyes.
If *you* don't care, at least spare *me* a little pain.
It breaks my mind. I die each time you put me wise
about your sins. My blood runs cold in every vein.
I love you and I try to hate you, but I can't
stop loving you. I wish that I were dead, but dead
with you. I'll ask no tricky questions, and I shan't
pursue what you conceal. I'll stay deceived instead.

And if I ever catch you *in flagrante*, say,
or catch some act of shamelessness in mid-offence,
then please deny quite clearly what was clear as day –
your words will cancel out the evidence of sense.

It won't be hard for you to gain a victory –
you only need to say: 'I didn't!' Do not grudge
that little phrase! You'll win your lawsuit easily,
if not through justice of your case, then through your judge.

Tacitus

Born 56/7 AD

Historian

Publius Cornelius Tacitus, the most brilliant and influential of imperial historians, writes here in his **magnum opus** 'The Annals of Imperial Rome' of the emperor Claudius, uncle and successor to Gaius Caligula, and his wife Valeria Messalina, whose name has become a byword for depravity. Claudius was a sympathetic but absurd figure, physically infirm and grotesque he had been kept from the public eye by his family, and was made emperor at the age of fifty by the Praetorians – the emperor's personal Guard – upon Caligula's assassination. Messalina, more than thirty years her husband's junior, bore him two children, Britannicus and Octavia, but became notorious for her viciousness and promiscuity. The trusting Claudius seems to have remained ignorant of his wife's true nature, until in AD 48 she made an extraordinary attempt to marry her lover, the consul-elect, Gaius Silius, and to wrest power from her husband.

TACITUS

from the *Annals*

XI, 25–38: The Death of Messalina, Wife of Claudius.

But now came the end of Claudius' blindness to what was happening in his own home. Before long he was forced to take notice of, and to punish his wife's excesses – only to be caught up after that in an incestuous marriage.

Messalina was by now finding adultery so easy that it bored her, and she was beginning to turn gradually towards more unusual libidinous practices, at which point her lover, Gaius Silius, started urging her that they should drop the pretence – either out of a deadly foolishness, or because he reckoned that the threat of danger was best countered by doing something dangerous oneself. He did not think that they needed to wait for old age to remove the emperor; planning was only innocent for those who were not actually guilty already, whereas manifest guilt needed the support of bold action. He was, he said, unmarried, childless, willing to marry, and prepared to adopt Britannicus; Messalina would keep the same powers as she had before, and would also have peace of mind if they could only get over the problem of Claudius, who, if slow on the uptake as far as deceit was concerned, was very quick-tempered. She listened to her lover's words without particular enthusiasm – not because of any love for her husband, but for fear that Silius, once he had reached the top, would then reject his mistress and come to see this crime, committed under pressure, for what it was. But for all that, she still wanted to be called 'wife,' simply because it *was* so massively wicked, wickedness for its own sake being the ultimate pleasure of the very bad. Therefore they waited only until Claudius had left for Ostia to make a religious sacrifice before they went through a full solemnization of their marriage.

I know it must seem amazing that any human beings could have felt safe doing something in a city where everybody knows all and tells all, especially when the something is this: a consul-designate and the emperor's wife get together before witnesses on a given day to celebrate a marriage 'for the procreation of children;' the woman listens to the auguries, puts on the bridal veil and sacrifices to the gods; they have a dinner with guests, kiss, and then spend the night together under the licence of matrimony. But I have added no extra touches; and what I shall tell you is truth as it was heard and written down by older men.

And so the imperial household shuddered, the chief secretaries more than anyone else; they were the ones most afraid of any change in the set-up, and they no longer whispered, but now said openly that when Mnester the actor had been defiling the emperor's bed, this might have been humiliating, but actual disaster had still been a long way off. But now a young and handsome nobleman, intelligent and about to take up a consulship, was preparing himself for something even better than that. It was hardly difficult to work out what would follow on from a marriage like this. They became very frightened indeed when they took into account Claudius's complete and utter subservience to his wife, and the many killings already ordered by Messalina. On the other hand, the fact that the emperor was easily swayed led them to hope that if they could get the upper hand by showing up the audacity of her crime, then they might manage to get her judged and condemned before she even came to trial. But everything hung on whether her defence was heard, and whether they could close Claudius's ears to her confession.

First of all the secretaries, Callistus (whom I mentioned earlier in the context of the killing of Caligula), Narcissus (who had contrived the murder of Silanus, Messalina's stepfather), and Pallas, who was at that time at the high point of his influence, all discussed whether they could still use undercover threats to make Messalina give up this love-affair with Silius, while pretending not to know any details. But Pallas and Callistus decided against acting, for fear that if they failed, it might lead to their own destruction – Pallas through cowardice, and Narcissus because he had learned under Caligula that caution was a better way of keeping power than precipitate action. Only Narcissus persisted, with the one modification that no-one should warn Messalina of the charge or the accuser. Narcissus waited for his chance while Claudius delayed at Ostia, and then persuaded two mistresses, with whom the emperor spent a lot of time, to go and tell him, using bribery and also promises of the greater powers that they would enjoy when his wife had fallen.

Next, one of these women, whose name was Calpurnia, was allowed to speak to him in private, threw herself at his feet and told him that Messalina had married Silius. Then she quickly asked the other woman, Cleopatra (who was standing by ready for this) whether she knew as well. When she agreed, Calpurnia asked for Narcissus to be sent for. He began by saying that he was sorry for having in the past pretended not to know about lovers like Vettius Valens or Plautius Lateranus; nor, indeed, would he now accuse Messalina of these adulteries, and would not even want to demand that she hand back Claudius's home, slaves and other imperial property. No, let the other man enjoy these things – but he *must* give Claudius back his wife and tear up the new marriage-contract! 'Did you know,' he asked, 'that you were divorced? The people, the Senate and the soldiers have all seen the marriage of Silius. If you don't act quickly, this "husband" will hold Rome!'

At this, the emperor summoned his closest friends and questioned first of all Turranius, the prefect in charge of the grain-supply, and after him Lucius Geta, the Praetorian commander. They confirmed what had happened, and others in the group told him to go to the camp and ensure the loyalty of the Praetorian Guard – to make sure about security before thinking of revenge. It is sufficiently well documented that Claudius, confused and terrified, kept on asking if he were emperor, and Silius a private citizen.

Messalina, meanwhile, had never indulged herself so much. It was well into autumn, so she was celebrating a mock wine-festival all round the palace. Wine-presses were working, the vats were overflowing, and women were dancing about dressed in animal-skins, as if they were Bacchantes in the frenzy of sacrifice to the wine-god. She herself was there with her hair loose, waving the vine-and-ivy staff of a Bacchante, accompanied by Silius, wearing the ivy crown and high boots of the god himself and tossing his head, while all around him a disreputable chorus was shouting away. The tale is told that Vettius Valens, who had climbed into a tall tree as a joke, was asked what he saw, and said that he saw a terrible storm over Ostia — either one really was brewing, or maybe this was just a chance phrase that turned out to be prophetic.

Meanwhile, not just rumours but also messengers were arriving from everywhere to say that Claudius knew everything and was on his way at top speed to get his revenge, therefore they split up, Messalina going to the Gardens of Lucullus, and Silius, to hide his own fear, to carry out his business in the Forum. The rest were slipping off in all directions when the centurions of the Guard caught them and put them in chains, some in the open, others when they were trying to hide. Messalina, unable to think clearly in these desperate circumstances, decided at once to meet and let herself be seen by her husband; this was a ploy that had helped her often in the past. She also sent word that Britannicus and Octavia should run and embrace their father. She also begged Vibidia, the most venerable of the Vestals, to speak to Claudius in his role as High Priest, and to beg for mercy. Then she, with only three companions (she had quickly been abandoned), crossed the entire city on foot, and then set off on the road towards Ostia in a cart that was used to take away garden rubbish. Nobody showed any sympathy for her — all that was cancelled out by the disgusting nature of her crimes.

Claudius himself was no less agitated. The Praetorian

commander, Geta, did not inspire complete confidence because he veered inconsistently between honest and wicked behaviour. For this reason Narcissus (supported by others who had the same fears) said that there was no hope of saving the emperor unless the command of the troops was transferred for that day only to one of the freedmen-secretaries, and he put himself forward for the task. And just in case Claudius might be induced to relent on the way back to the city by his friends Lucius Vitellius and Gaius Caecina Largus, Narcissus demanded – and got – a seat in the carriage with them.

The story was widely told after the events that the emperor kept saying different things, cursing the wanton behaviour of his wife at one moment, and at the next reminiscing about his marriage, and his children when they were babies. Vitellius wouldn't say anything except 'Oh, what a crime! Oh, how wicked!' Narcissus pressed him to spell it out and tell the truth, but to no avail, since he answered by saying things that could be taken either way. Caecina Largus did the same.

Now Messalina came into sight and shouted to the emperor to listen to the mother of Britannicus and Octavia. But her accuser, Narcissus, shouted out the story of Silius and the marriage, and as he did so gave Claudius a written account of all her debaucheries, to keep his attention away from Messalina herself. A little while later, when they were about to enter Rome, the children tried to come forward, but Narcissus ordered their removal from the scene. He could not rebuff Vibidia, however, who demanded with great anger that a wife should not be condemned to death without offering a defence. So Narcissus said that the emperor would hear her, that she would be able to answer the charge, and that the Vestal should go and see to her religious duties.

Claudius was strangely silent through all this, and Lucius Vitellius looked as if he didn't know what was going on at all. The freedman Narcissus was in charge. He gave orders that the house of the adulterous Silius should be thrown open, and that the emperor should be taken there. First of all he drew attention to a statue of Silius's father in the entrance hall – statues of him had been banned by the Senate – and then to the various heirlooms of the Julio-Claudian family that had been given in payment for wickedness. Narcissus now took Claudius, who had become very worked up and had started issuing threats, to the Praetorian Camp, where an assembly of the soldiers was waiting. Narcissus gave an opening statement, and then Claudius made a brief speech only, because although he was justifiably saddened, he was too ashamed to put it into words. The Praetorians then shouted continuously for the names of the offenders and that their crimes should be punished. Silius was brought before the tribunal, but offered no defence and asked for no stay of execution, begging them to kill him quickly. This steadfast attitude was imitated by various other Roman nobles, who also asked for a quick death. Titius Proculus, whom Silius had made a kind of official 'guardian' of Messalina, now gave evidence and was condemned, as was Vettius Valens, who confessed, and their colleagues Pompeius Urbicus and Saufeius Trogus. The same sentence was pronounced on Decrius Calpurnius, captain of the watch, on Sulpicius Rufus, impressario of the gladiatorial games, and on the senator Juncus Vergilianus.

Only the actor Mnester slowed the proceedings down when he tore open his clothes and shouted that Claudius should look at the weals he had received, and should remember that he had said that Mnester should carry out Messalina's orders. Others had acted out of greed, or in hope of advancement, but he had been forced. Also, he would have been the first to go if Silius had gained power. The emperor was moved by this and inclined to mercy, but the freedmen-secretaries persuaded him that, after having so many noblemen killed, he should not spare a mere Thespian, and that whether the act was voluntary or forced was irrelevant given the magnitude of the crime. Nor was the defence of a Roman noble called Traulus

Montanus accepted. He was a modest and good-looking young man, and had been summoned and dismissed by Messalina, who was equally fickle in her likes and dislikes, on one single night. The death sentence was remitted for Suillius Caesoninus and Plautius Lateranus, the latter because of the distinguished service of his father's brother, Plautius Silvanus. Suillius Caesoninus was protected by his own vices – in the disgusting festivities he had only played the woman's part.

Meanwhile, in the Gardens of Lucullus, Messalina, fighting for her life, was composing a petition in hope and sometimes even in indignation – she still retained that old arrogance, even *in extremis*. If Narcissus, moreover, had not hurried up the process of getting her killed, things could have turned fatally on Narcissus himself. Claudius was back at home, feeling better after an early dinner and warmed by the wine, and now ordered someone to go and tell 'that poor woman' (those are the exact words he is said to have used) to come and defend herself on the following day.

When they heard this they began to worry that his anger might fade away and his love return, especially if during the night he started having bedroom thoughts about his wife, so Narcissus rushed out and told a tribune of the guard, who was there with some centurions, to go and kill her, telling him that the emperor had given the command. Another freedman, Evodus, was sent to keep watch and to make sure that it was done. He got to the Gardens very quickly, and found Messalina prostrate, with her mother, Domitia Lepida beside her. When her daughter had been at the height of her power Lepida had been put aside, but now she had taken pity on Messalina in her hour of need, and was advising her to kill herself before someone else did so. Messalina's life was over, she said, and she should at least choose a decent death. But there was no honour in that vice-ridden soul, and she kept on weeping and asking useless questions until the doors burst open and the group rushed in. The tribune stood silent in front of her, while the freedman hurled slave-language abuse at her.

Now she saw her fate clearly for the first time, and took the dagger. Trembling with fear, she put it to her throat and then to her breast, but all without doing anything, so the tribune stabbed her. Her mother was allowed to keep the body. It was reported to Claudius that Messalina had died, although it was not made clear whether it was by her own or someone else's hand. Nor did he ask; he called for wine and got on with dinner in the normal way. In the next few days he gave no signs of hatred or of joy, anger or sadness or any other human emotion – neither when he saw the freedmen celebrating, nor when he saw his children mourning. This loss of memory was helped by the Senate, which called for the name and any statues of Messalina to be removed from private and public places. Narcissus was made honorary quaestor, the last contribution to the pride of a man who rose higher than either Pallas or Callistus.

The whole business had been necessary, but the long-term consequences were dire.

Tacitus

The Murder of Claudius

The 'dire consequences' that Tacitus mentions following the death of Messalina were the incestuous marriage of Claudius to his own niece, Agrippina, and the subsequent adoption by Claudius of her son by a previous marriage, the later emperor Nero. As time passed, however, Claudius tired of the turbulent and power-hungry Agrippina, and grew reconciled to his own young son by Messalina, Britannicus. Agrippina saw that if Nero was to succeed her husband as emperor she must act at once.

XII, 66–69: THE MURDER OF CLAUDIUS

Agrippina, who had long since decided on murder, and who certainly wasn't lacking in assistants, was now ready to seize her chance, and so she took advice on types of poison. Something drastic and too quick would give away the deed. If she chose something slow and wasting, then Claudius, faced with death and aware of her malice, might start to love his son, Britannicus, again. Her best chance was with something subtle, which would disturb his mind whilst producing a gradual demise. A real expert in the field was chosen, a woman called Locusta, who had been condemned for poisoning, but was kept alive for a long time since she was very useful to anyone ruling the empire. The skills of this woman produced a potion which the eunuch Halotus, whose job was to serve and taste the food, gave to Claudius.

Later on, the whole story came out, and writers of the time have stated that poison was added to an especially tasty mushroom, though it was not felt by Claudius right away, either because of his general sluggishness or because he was drunk; furthermore, evacuating his bowels seemed to have saved him. In consequence, Agrippina became very frightened, but when worse outcomes are feared, who worries about immediate danger? She had already arranged for, and now used the complicity of the doctor, Xenophon. He is believed to have put a feather, dipped in rapid-acting poison, down Claudius' throat while pretending to help him vomit. He was hardly unaware of the fact that the most wicked of crimes are dangerous to undertake, but very profitable, once carried out.

Meanwhile the Senate was called together and the consuls and priests were offering prayers for the safety of the emperor at the same time as his already lifeless body was being wrapped in blankets and covered with poultices, and as measures were being taken to ensure the succession of Nero. First of all, Agrippina, apparently heartbroken and wanting to be comforted, clasped hold of Britannicus and said that he was the very image of his father, and by this and other tricks she prevented him from leaving his room. She also held back his sisters Antonia and Octavia, and closed off all means of access by posting her guards. She issued frequent public bulletins to the effect that emperor's health was improving, which kept up the hopes of the Praetorian Guard, while she waited for the auspicious time promised by the astrologers.

Then at midday on October 13th, the palace gates were thrown open and Nero rode out, accompanied by the Praetorian Prefect, Sextus Burrus, to the guards who were there on official duty. Then, at a word from the Prefect, Nero was lifted amid cheers into a litter. It is said that some men were doubtful, and looked back and asked where Britannicus was. But soon, when no alternative lead had been given, they also followed. Having been carried into the Praetorian Camp, Nero then promised, after a few suitable prefatory comments, an accession gift matching the generosity of his adoptive father, Claudius, and he was acclaimed by the soldiers, who used the imperial title. The acclaim of the Praetorians was followed by senatorial edicts, and there was no hesitation in the provinces. Divine honours were voted to Claudius, and the funeral solemnities were based on those held for the divine Augustus, with Agrippina imitating the magnificence of her great-grandmother, Livia. The will, however, was not read, in case the preference of stepson over son should create in the popular mind any impression of injustice or invidious behaviour.

Seneca

Died AD 65

Stoic Philosopher and Statesman

That Nero was privy to Claudius' murder was demonstrated by a joke he made on one occasion at dinner, when he declared that 'mushrooms are the food of gods'. The point being that following his death – by way of a mushroom – Claudius was granted divine honours, deified as a god of the Roman state as Julius Caesar and Augustus had also been following their deaths. Presumably it was Agrippina herself who instigated or inspired this posthumous honour the Senate voted her husband, to elevate her own prestige and that of the dynasty.

At Claudius' funeral, Nero delivered an elegant eulogy in praise of his predecessor. It was written by Nero's tutor and adviser, Lucius Annaeus Seneca the younger. It was also Seneca who wrote the following work, the **Apocolocyntosis** or The Deification of Claudius, to privately amuse and flatter Nero, with its venomous and satirical account of the arrival of the doddering 'god' Claudius in Heaven.

SENECA

The Apocolocyntosis,

or: *The High Drama of Claudius the Gourd*

I wish to write down an account for posterity of what
happened in heaven on last October 13th, the beginning of
this most prosperous age. It shall be written without any
bias whatsoever. This is the absolute truth. If the reader
wants to ask how I know these things, first of all I shall not
answer if I don't want to. Who is going to force me? I
know that I have been a free man ever since the day he
died, thereby proving true the saying that 'you have to be
born either a king or a fool.' If I should wish to answer, I
shall say the first thing that comes into my head. Who has
ever managed to get actual witnesses out of an historian?
However, if it *is* necessary to produce witnesses, ask the
man who saw Caligula's sister Drusilla going up to heaven;
that very man will swear that he saw the emperor Claudius
on the same road, though, to quote Vergil, 'tripping with
much smaller steps.' Whether he likes it or not, he has to
keep an eye on all that happens in heaven. He is the Appian
Way guard, the road (as I'm sure you know) by which
both Augustus and Tiberius Caesar went to the gods. If
you were to question him, he will talk to you – in private.
But in company he will keep mum. Because ever since that
time when he swore in the Senate that he had seen Drusilla
going up to heaven and no one believed all his good news,
he has solemnly stated that he will never reveal what he has
seen, even if he were to witness a man murdered in public.
And so, I am writing down accurately and precisely the
story I have heard, and I hope that he is fit and well. So,

Phoebus his chariot on the shorter route had flown,
the hours of dark and sleep had therefore lengthy grown,
and all the kingdoms had become Diana's own.
Autumn had fallen prey to ugly winter's greed,
that Bacchus should become an old man was decreed,
and people rushed to get the last grapes in with speed.

But I think that I shall be understood better if I explain
that the month was October and that it was the 13th. I'm
not exactly sure about the time, it is easier to get philosophers to agree than clocks — at any rate it was sometime
between noon and one. Rather provincial, perhaps? But all
the poets are in agreement: unhappy just to describe dawn
and dusk, they are now disturbing the middle of the day.
Will *you* pass over such a good hour? I hear you say. No.

For now had Phoebus reached the middle of his course,
and, slightly nearer night than day, reined in his horse
to lead the fiery orb back downwards to its source.

Claudius was at death's door, but he couldn't find the
doorknob. Then the god Mercury, who had always enjoyed Claudius's wit, quietly took Clotho, one of the three
Fates, to one side and said: 'Look, you bitch, why are you
allowing this miserable man to be tormented. After all of
this torture, can't he have a break? It's been 64 years since
he started to gasp for breath. What do you have against
him and his country? Let the fortune tellers be right for
once in their lives. Ever since he became emperor they
have been trying to bury him every month and every year.
And it's no wonder that they're wrong and that no one
can predict his last hour — frankly no-one *really* knew that
he had ever been born. Do what has to be done, just like it
says in the *Georgics:* 'kill him, and put his better on his
empty throne.' But Clotho said, 'For Hercules' sake! I
wanted to give him a little *more* time, to let him give
citizenship to the few people left without it (he'd already
decided to see all the Greeks, Gauls, Spaniards and Britons
in togas). But the idea rather appeals of leaving a few

foreigners aside as seed, and, since you order it, well, so be it.' She opened her casket and brought out three spindles: one was for addled Augurinus, the second for babbling Baba, and the third was for C-for-Claudius. 'I will make these three die in one year at short intervals, and I won't send him on his own. It isn't right for him to be suddenly left alone, used as he was to seeing so many thousand following him, with as many again in front of him and as many around him. He will be happy with these temporary companions.'

She spoke, and winds the thread onto the dumpy spool,
and snips the lifeline shorter of the royal fool.

And then Lachesis, hair ornate upon her head,
her brow adorned with garlands and with laurel band,
teases out from the gleaming wool a snow-white thread,
which changes colour 'neath her fine and skilful hand.
Her sisters gaze at her with wonder in their eyes
as ordinary wool is changed to purest gold,
a filament that runs through all the centuries.
In sheer delight they now the happy fleeces hold,
loving to fill their hands with that delightful wool,
to do a job that almost does itself! The gold
thread falls, fine and well-twisted, running from the spool
for more years even than the oldest of the old.

Phoebus Apollo now rejoices in his song,
as happily upon his well-tuned harp he plays
the melodies that help his sisters' work along;
and while they spin, their brother's tuneful songs they praise.

So rapt are they, they spin more than a man is due,
but then Apollo says: 'O Fates, my sisters dear,
take not an extra day away from this one mortal, who
is peer to me in singing and in beauty clear.
He'll make the rolling years seem noble, fair and bright;
he'll bring to life again the ancient laws, the best.

Just like the Morning Star, he'll put the night to flight,
and like the Evening Star he'll outshine all the rest.
Just as at rosy dawn the sun illuminates
earth's orb, riding his fiery car, so Caesar too
looks forth with splendour in his face on Rome's estate,
and Nero's glance lights up the city, fair to view,
while on his neck the tumbling locks fall down anew.

Thus spake Apollo. And Lachesis, the second of the Fates, who was favourably disposed towards any handsome man, gave out with a generous hand and slipped Nero many years. They all ordered however, that Claudius, exactly as Euripides put it, should 'be carried out by mourners with a happy and a holy reverence.' Then his soul bubbled up and he clearly ceased to be alive. When he died, however, he was listening to a group of comedians, so you can see that my horror of those types is not without cause. His last words heard on earth were these – with a loud noise coming from the end of him that communicated most easily, he said, 'oh deary me. I think I've shat myself.' I don't know whether he did or not, but he certainly shat on everything else.

It is a waste of time to relate what happened afterwards on earth. You know very well what happened and there is no danger of forgetting the impression made by public rejoicing on the memory. No one is going to forget their own happiness. Listen, this is what happened in heaven – for more details, ask my source. It was brought to Jupiter's attention that a well built gentleman with whitish-grey hair had arrived. He seemed to be threatening something, for he kept shaking his head and was dragging his right foot. Questioned what country he was from, he gibbered something in a confused mumble – they did not understand his language. He wasn't Greek, Roman or any known race.

Then Jupiter suggested that Hercules, who had travelled the whole world and seemed to know every nation, go and find out where he came from. Hercules was badly shaken at the first glimpse of him, even though he wasn't scared of any monster. When he saw this new type of creature with its strange way of walking, and a voice of no earthly animal – more like a very large sea monster, it was so hoarse and confused – he thought that he was going into his thirteenth labour. When he looked closer, it did seem to be some kind of man. Therefore he went up to it and asked in Homer's language (since it was easiest for him to speak in Greek):

'who are you, of what race, and where your place on earth?'

Claudius was pleased that there were literary men there and hoped that there would be a niche for his own *Histories*. And so, to show that he was Caesar, he himself used a line from Homer:

'The breeze blew me from Ilium to Thracian shores.'

The line after that one, however, was more appropriate, and equally Homeric:

'Where I destroyed the city and killed all the men.'

And he would have put one over on Hercules, who is a little slow, if the Goddess of Fever had not been there. She was the only one to leave her temple and come with him – he had left all of the others in Rome: 'This man is telling you nothing but lies,' she said. 'I'll tell you the truth because I've lived with him all these years. He was born in Lyons. You have before you one of Mark Antony's townsmen. As I say, he was born sixteen miles from Vienne, so he's a thoroughbred Gaul. And so, just like the Gauls are supposed to do, he captured Rome. I assure you that he was born in Lyons, where that extortionist Licinus ruled for many years. You've tramped over more places than any professional muleteer, so you ought to know the people of Lyons, and also that there are many miles between the Scamander and the Rhone.'

At this point Claudius lost his temper and showed his

anger as loudly as he could. No one understood what he was saying. In actual fact, he was ordering that Madam Fever be taken away, and making that sign with his shaking hand – steady enough for this one thing, however, when he used to cut men's heads off. What he had ordered was 'off with her head,' but you would have thought that they were all his own freedmen, for all the notice they took of him.

'Listen to me,' said Hercules then. 'Stop playing the fool. You have come to a place where even the mice nibble iron! Out with the truth, or I'll knock this nonsense out of you.' And to make himself more terrifying, he said in the manner of a tragic actor:

> 'Come tell me sir, what birthplace do you claim,
> or else I'll use this club to strike you down,
> a club with which great kings have been despatched!
> Why do you gibber, squeak and make no sense?
> What land or race produced that nodding head?
> Once, when I went to seek the threefold king
> and from the far Hesperides, I drove
> his cattle to the noble land of Greece,
> I saw a mountain, where two rivers flow,
> where Phoebus' chariot daily gazes down
> upon the mighty Rhone's fast-flowing stream,
> and where the Saône, unsure which way to take,
> with quiet ripples gently rolls along –
> is *that* the land which gave you to the world?

He declaimed these lines with a fair amount of spirit and gusto. All the same, he was not quite in control, and slightly worried about being struck down by the Wrath of Clod. Claudius, when he saw the size of him, forgot his frivolities and realised that although no one was his equal in Rome, here he didn't have quite the same standing – Chanteclere is worth most of all in his own dunghill. As far as it was possible to understand, this is what he seemed to say: 'I did hope that you would stand up for me against the others, Hercules, bravest of the gods. If I needed someone to vouch for me, I was going to name you, as you know me the best. If you remember, right through July and August I used to pass judgement in court before your temple. You know what misery I went through there, listening to lawyers day and night. If you had come across these people, however brave you think you are, you would have preferred to clean up the Augean sewers. I had to put up with a lot more shit than you did. But since I want . . .'

[There follows a lacuna of several pages. It would appear that Claudius manages to convince Hercules, who takes up his cause in the Senate. There the matter of Claudius's deification is debated, with Claudius himself present at first, although he is removed on the 'I spy strangers' rule later on.]

'It's not surprising that you could force your way into the Senate – nothing is barred to you. Just tell us, what kind of god you wish him to be made. He can't be an Epicurean god, 'for they don't bother us, nor we see them.' A Stoic god? How can he be 'quite round,' as the philosopher Varro says, 'and quite without a foreskin or a head?' I can see now there *is* something of a Stoic god in him – he doesn't have either a heart or a head. If, Hercules help us, he'd asked this favour from Saturn, he wouldn't have got it, even though he celebrated his festival the whole year round, like a truly Saturnalian emperor. Nor is he going to get it from Jupiter, whom he condemned for incest (insofar as he could). Well, he killed his son-in-law Silanus because the man had a sister – the most charming girl in the world – whom all called Venus. He preferred to call her Juno. Why? I hear you ask. Why his own sister? All I can say is: do your homework, stupid! You can go half-way in Athens and all the way in Alexandria. Just because in Rome you tell me the cats always get the cream, does that mean that this person can straighten things out up here with us? I have no idea what he does in his bedroom, and now he is keeping his eyes peeled for lands in heaven. He wants to become a god. Is it not enough that he has a temple in Britain where barbarians revere him and pray 'Clod have mercy on our souls?'

At last Jupiter remembered that it was not permitted to propose or oppose a motion with members of the public in the House. 'Honourable members,' he said. 'I gave you permission to ask questions, but you have turned this place into a veritable bear-garden. I must ask you to observe standing orders. What will this person think of us, whoever he might be?' Claudius was sent out, and the first person to be asked his opinion was Father Janus. He had been made consul-elect from the first afternoon in July and was as shrewd a character as you could want, because he could always see before and behind at the same time. Because he lived in the Forum, he made an eloquent speech, which the secretary could not keep up with. I am therefore not going to try and repeat it verbatim, in case I change the actual words he used. He said much about the greatness of the gods and that it wasn't an honour that ought to be dished out to the proles. 'Once upon a time,' he said. 'It was a great thing to become a god. Now you have made it worth less than tuppence. Therefore, so that it doesn't look as though I am speaking against just this one case rather than the principle of the thing, I move that from this day on, divinity be not granted to any of those who, as Homer says, 'eat of the fruits provided by the earth,' or those nurtured by Mother Nature. Anyone then who, in contravention of this bill, is declared a god, spoken of as a god or portrayed as a god shall be handed over to the Chief Devils, and at the next public games shall be flogged with the new recruits.'

The next person asked was the son of the goddess Vica Pota, Pluto, god of the underworld and of wealth, also consul-elect and a moneylender. He made his living that way, and had a sideline in selling citizenships. Hercules shimmied up to him and touched him on the ear to remind him that he was speaking for the motion. Pluto expressed his opinion with these words: 'as the divine Claudius is a blood relative of both the divine Augustus and also his godmother, the divine Livia Augusta – whom he personally ordered deified – and as he is brighter than all mortals, and as it will be to the benefit of the state to have another who can 'eat his turnips with a will' together with Romulus, I propose that the divine Claudius be made a god from today, and that he be given the honour with as much right as anyone before him. Further, that a note of the matter be inserted into Ovid's *Metamorphoses*.'

Opinion was divided, and it looked as though Claudius was going to win. For Hercules, who saw that his irons were in the fire, rushed here and there and kept saying: 'don't turn me down. I'm putting my neck on the block here. I'll do the same for you next time you want a favour. You scratch my back and I'll scratch yours.'

Then the divine Augustus got to his feet when his turn to speak came, and he debated with the greatest eloquence. 'Honourable members,' he said, 'I have you as witnesses that since I was made a god, I have never said a word. I always mind my own business. But I cannot ignore this any longer or hide the grief which my conscience makes all the greater. Was it for this that I brought peace to land and sea? That I put a stop to the civil war? That I introduced laws to Rome and made the city beautiful with buildings, too – I cannot find the words, honourable members. No words can equal my indignation. I must therefore fall back on the words of Valerius Messala Corvinus, that most eloquent gentleman, and say 'I am ashamed of my authority.' Gentlemen, this person before you, who seems incapable of hurting a fly, killed men as easily as a dog pisses. But why am I talking to you about all these nameless men? There is no time to cry over national disasters when we are contemplating private sorrows. I shall therefore pass over the former, and say only this – for I know Greek, even if my sister doesn't, and charity begins at home! This man you see here, who for so many years has been hiding under my name, did me the favour of killing the two Julias, my granddaughters. One he put to the sword, the other he starved. And a grandson too, Lucius Silanus. You will see, Jupiter, if he had a valid case there – it is definitely one for you to consider, if you are to be fair. Tell me, divine Claudius, why did you condemn all those you killed before you knew the charges and before you heard their defence? Where on earth do people do things that way? It doesn't happen in heaven. Look at Jupiter, who has ruled all these years. Only in the case of Vulcan did he cause him to break his leg, when he

> 'caught him by the heel,
> and hurled him from the holy threshold down!'

as Homer puts it. And he was once angry with his wife and hung her up. But did he kill her? *You* killed Messalina, and I was her great-uncle just as much as I was yours. You didn't know about it, you say? Damn you! Ignorance is worse than killing. He went on harrassing Caligula, even after he was dead. Caligula murdered his father-in-law, Claudius killed his son-in-law as well. Caligula wouldn't let Crassus's son, Pompey, keep the surname 'the Great.' Claudius gave him his name back and took his head instead. In one household alone, he killed Licinius Crassus Frugi, his wife Scribonia and his son Pompey, called Magnus. Fools maybe, but they *were* aristocrats; in fact, Crassus was such a great fool that he might even have made emperor. And this is the man you want to be made a god? Look at his body, disliked by the gods since birth. All right, let him say three clear words one after the other, and then he can drag me off as a slave. Who is going to worship him as a god? Who will believe in him? No one is going to believe that *you* are gods, if you make gods out of people like him. In conclusion, gentlemen, if I have lived as an honourable man while I was with you, if I never insulted anybody, then avenge my wrongs. Honourable members, I move.' Then he read from a notebook: 'in as much as the divine Claudius murdered his father-in-law Appius Silanus, his two sons-in-law Pompey Magnus and Lucius Silanus, his daughter's father-in-law Crassus

Frugi – a man as identical to him as two peas in a pod – his daughter's mother-in-law Scribonia, his wife Messalina and others too numerous to mention, I propose that he be severely punished, that he be given no stay of judgement, and that he be instantly banished and leave heaven within thirty days and Olympus within three.'

The noes had it. Without delay, Mercury grabbed Claudius by the scruff of his neck and dragged him from heaven to hell, 'the place from which no traveller returns.'

While they were going down the Sacred Way, Mercury asked what was that crowd in front? Was it Claudius's funeral procession? It was a most beautiful sight, with no expense spared so you knew that a god was being buried. Such a noise of trumpeters, horn players and all kinds of brass instruments that even Claudius could hear. Everyone was happy and cheerful, the people of Rome walking around as if they were free. Agatho and a few barristers were crying, but this time it was clearly meant. The barristers were coming out of their dingy corners – pale and thin and with hardly a breath in their bodies. They were like men coming to life again. One, when he saw the barristers huddled together weeping over their fate, went up and said: 'I did say that the party wouldn't last for ever.' When Claudius saw his own funeral he twigged that he was dead. For a huge choir was singing his requiem in rhymed quatrains:

> Weep and wail and tear your hair,
> let the sounds of sorrow fall,
> for he is dead, the best, most fair,
> the noblest caesar of them all.

> Swifter than a horse in flight
> trampler of the rebels' head,
> Persians, Parthians felt his might,
> at his arrows how they fled!

> Just a single shot, no more,
> brought painted Medes under his sway,

or Britons on their distant shore,
or woad-soaked Celts who soon gave way.

He brought the lot of them back home
in chains, but gave the law as well,
to everyone, a brave new Rome,
and tamed the mighty ocean's swell.

Weep for this man, the swiftest to
judge cases, when he'd heard a part,
and it was only half-way through
(or sometimes well before the start!)

Now on the bench who's left behind
to work all year, now he's below?
Minos, Judge of the Dead, be kind,
You'll have to yield your seat, you know!

You legal quibblers, tear your hair,
you poetasters, too. Wail, gnash
your teeth, you con-men everywhere,
whose dodgy dice rake in the cash.

Claudius was delighted to hear his praises sung and wanted
to watch for longer. But the divine herald of the gods
grabbed him and dragged him across the Campus Martius,
first covering his head so that no one would recognise him.
Somewhere between the River Tiber and the Via Tecta he
went down to hell. Claudius' freedman, Narcissus, had
gone down to hell before him, taking a short cut with his
own hand, so he could be there to welcome his master. He
met him all glistening, because he had just got out of the
bath, and asked, 'What are the gods doing with men?'
'Hurry up,' replied Mercury, 'and announce our new
arrival.' Narcissus flew off quicker than a flash. It's an easy
descent, as it's downhill all the way. Therefore, although
he had the gout, he came in a moment to the gate of Dis.
There lay Cerberus, or as Horace puts it, 'the hundred
headed monster.' He was a little worried when he saw the
black, shaggy dog – he'd only ever had an off-white

90

mongrel as a pet. It was not the kind of dog you wished to meet in the dark. In a loud voice he said, 'Claudius is coming!' With much clapping, people went ahead singing in Greek: 'He that was lost is found, therefore let us rejoice.'

There was Gaius Silius, consul-elect, the praetor Juncus, Sextus Traulus Marcus Helvius, Trogus, Cotta, Vettius Valens, Fabius and the Roman knights that Narcissus had ordered executed. In the middle of this singing crowd was Mnester the actor – the one Claudius had cut down to size because of his looks. The news spread quickly that Claudius had arrived and they all milled around Messalina: first of all his freedmen Polybius, Myron, Harpocras, Amphaeus and Pheronactus. Claudius had sent all of these ahead of him so that he would be attended wherever he went. Then came the two prefects, Justus Catonius and Rufrius Pollio; then his friends Saturninus Lusius and Pedo Pompeius, Lupus and Celer Asinius – both of consular standing. Finally his brother's daughter, his sister's daughter, sons-in-law, fathers and mothers-in-law – in fact all of his blood relatives. As one they came to meet Claudius and when he saw them he cried out: 'the place is full of friends,' – he said that in Greek –, then: 'how did you all get here?' Then Pedo Pompeius answered: 'What do you mean, you utter bastard? How did we get here? Who else sent us here but you? You murderer of all of your friends. I'll see you in court. I'll show you the bench down here.'

He led him to the tribunal of Aeacus, judge of the dead, who in hell presides over cases according to the Cornelian laws relating to murder. Pedo asked that Claudius' name be taken down; and asked for the following charges to be taken into consideration: thirty five senators and two hundred and twenty one Roman knights – all murdered, plus others 'as plentiful as grains of sand upon the shore.' Claudius couldn't find someone to speak for him. At last Publius Petronius, an old sidekick and master of the Claudian style, came forward and demanded the right of reply. Denied.

Pedo Pompeius opened for the prosecution, to great cheers. The counsel for the defense wished to reply. Aeacus turned down the request with complete impartiality, and having heard only one side of the case, passed sentence. 'As he did unto others, so let it be done unto him. My will be done.' There was utter silence. Everyone was struck dumb, shocked by this novel turn of affairs. They had never known anything like this before. To Claudius himself it seemed more unfair than unfamiliar. There was a long discussion about what sort of punishment he ought to endure. Some said that Sisyphus had carried stones long enough, others that Tantalus would die of thirst unless relieved, and others that a brake ought to be put on poor old Ixion's wheel. But it was determined that none of these old-timers be pardoned, in case Claudius hoped that something similar might ever happen to him. It was agreed that a new punishment be thought up – some senseless task that would raise desire without any effect. Then Aeacus ordered him to rattle dice in a tumbler with a hole in it. Straight away he began to look for eternally falling dice, getting absolutely nowhere.

> Time and again he shakes the little cup,
> but every time the dice fall on the floor;
> he'll try again when he has picked then up,
> but every time would be just like before.
> And so he searches for his dice, but no!
> they slip and slide and thus his fingers mock;
> it's just the same as happens down below
> with Sisyphus and his eternal rock.

Suddenly Caligula turned up and claimed him as his slave. He produced witnesses who said they had seen Claudius being flogged, beaten and generally cudgelled by Caligula in the past. The court found in favour of Caligula, who gave him to Judge Aeacus. He gave him to his freedman, Menander, to be his personal assistant.

Tacitus

The Fall of Agrippina

The achievement of her life's ambition in her son's imperial
elevation seems to have removed all traces of restraint from
Agrippina's nature. But her harsh and domineering ways
soon began to alienate Nero. His liaison with a beautiful
freedwoman, Acte, was used by Seneca and Burrus, his
principal advisers, to put further strife and distance between
the emperor and his mother. Frantic at her growing loss of
power and influence, Agrippina appears to have become
increasingly unbalanced. Her attempts to threaten Nero by
showing support for Claudius' son Britannicus led to the
sudden death of Britannicus while dining at the emperor's
table – supposedly by poison. Her attempts to regain her
psychological ascendancy became ever more threatening or
scandalous, until finally in AD 59 Nero decided they could
be tolerated no longer.

XIV, 3–8: THE FALL OF AGRIPPINA

The historian Cluvius Rufus tells us that Agrippina's desire to maintain her influential position went so far that at midday, when Nero was usually warm and relaxed from wine and food, she frequently offered herself to the tipsy emperor, dressed up and ready for incest. Soon, passionate kisses and endearments, signs of impending licentiousness, were noticed by those closest to them. Seneca, aiming to counter her feminine wiles by using another female, brought in a freedwoman called Acte, who, although frightened for herself and aware of Nero's terrible reputation, was to make known to him that his mother was glorying in the incest, and that the soldiers would not tolerate this kind of sacrilege in the ruler of the empire. Another historian of the period, Fabius Rusticus, says that it was Nero who wanted it rather than Agrippina, although he does note that it was indeed broken up by the cleverness of that same freedwoman. Other authorities agree with Cluvius's version, however, so that the balance of probability is on that side. Possibly the whole thing *was* a brainchild of Agrippina's; or perhaps the idea of such a novel lust was simply assumed to be more believable in a woman who had, for the sake of power, had a sexual relationship with Marcus Aemilius Lepidus when she was only a young girl, who had, for similar reasons, become the mistress of Claudius' secretary, Pallas, and who had indulged in every kind of moral turpitude by the fact of her marriage to Claudius himself, who was her uncle on her father's side.

Nero, therefore, began to avoid being alone with her, and when she went to her gardens, or to her estates at Tusculum or Antium he praised her intention of going away for a rest. Eventually he decided that she was a liability wherever she was, and decided to kill her, speculating further on whether he should do so by poison, the knife or some other means. The first choice was poison. But if it were given to her at an imperial dinner it would be difficult to claim it as ill-luck, since Britannicus had already gone that way. It also seemed difficult to bribe the servants of a woman who was used to crime, and always on the look-out for it. Besides, she had strengthened her body by taking remedies for poisons on a pre-emptive basis. No-one knew of a way of hiding a sword, or could come up with a similar way of cutting her down, and there was also the fear that anyone ordered to do the bloody deed would not actually do it. An ingenious idea came, however, from the freedman Anicetus, who had been a naval prefect at Misenum, the naval base on the Bay of Naples. He had been one of Nero's teachers when the emperor was a boy, and his hatred of Agrippina was reciprocated. He showed that it was possible to construct a ship of which a part could be designed to come away when they were already out at sea, and thus throw in the unsuspecting Agrippina. Nothing, Anicetus explained, is potentially more dangerous than a sea-journey, and if the lady were done away with by shipwreck, who would be malicious enough to see human wickedness in the misdeeds of the winds and the waves? The emperor would, after all, then set up a temple, altars and so forth, with a great show of piety for the dead Agrippina.

This seemed like a good plan, and the time was right as well, since Nero was in the habit of celebrating the festival of Minerva, in late March, at Baiae, and so he persuaded his mother to come there. He announced that from time to time one had to allow for parental outbursts, and that he proposed to show an understanding and placatory attitude. In this way he wanted to create an air of reconciliation, so that Agrippina, with the easy credulity of women for good news, would accept. She came, and Nero met her on the shore when she arrived from Antium, gave her his hand and embraced her, and then esorted her to Bauli – this was the name of a villa on the Bay, between the promontory of Misenum and the Lake of Baiae. Among the ships was one that was more finely decorated, another compliment to his mother, who was usually conveyed in a trireme with oarsmen from the navy. Then she was invited to Baiae for dinner (so that night might conceal the crime). It is well enough known that there was an informer, and Agrippina, when she heard, was in two minds whether or not to believe what she had heard, but she went to Baiae in a litter. Once there, however, her fears gave way under the attentions of Nero – she was made welcome and given the seat of honour. After a lot of talk – sometimes with the familiarity of a child, at others apparently serious – Nero saw her off, gazing into her eyes and pressing her tightly to himself, either as a final pretence, or perhaps because this last look at his doomed mother had affected even Nero's brutish nature.

But the gods seemed to have sent a starlit night and a calm and quiet sea, so that the wicked act would be witnessed. The ship had not travelled very far, and two of Agrippina's household were with her; one of them, Crep-ereius Gallus, was standing a little way from the tiller, while Acceronia was sitting at Agrippina's feet as she lay on a couch. They were reminiscing with delight about the penitent behaviour of Agrippina's son and her restoral to favour, when suddenly at a signal the canopy over them (which was weighted with lead) fell down and crushed Crepereius to death immediately. Agrippina and Acceronia were protected by the high sides of the couch, which happened to be able to resist the weight. Nor, indeed, did the ship collapse, and in the chaos those that knew what was going on were impeded by the large numbers of these who did not. Then the oarsmen decided to throw all their weight onto one side and capsize the ship that way. However, there was no instant agreement on this emergency move, and the fact that others were working in the opposite direction allowed people to drop into the sea less abruptly. Acceronia unwisely shouted out that she was Agrippina, and that someone should help the mother of the emperor, and was immediately killed by blows from stanchions, oars and any other ship's equipment that came to hand. Agrippina kept quiet and was therefore not recognized, although she did receive one wound in the shoulder; she swam away until she met some small fishing-boats and was brought to the Lucrine Lake, and then back to her villa.

There, she gave some thought to the treacherous invitation and to the more-than-special way she had been treated, and also to the fact that they had not been far away from the shore, and that the ship, which hadn't been buffetted by the winds and hadn't run onto rocks, had still fallen apart from the top downwards, like something built on land that was designed to do just that. When she took into account the death of Acceronia and also her own wound, she realised that her only defence against this treachery was not to acknowledge it. So she sent Agermus, a freedman, to tell her son that by divine grace and to his good fortune she had been saved from a serious accident, but that she implored him not to come and see her yet, however anxious about the danger in which his mother had been, because at the moment she needed rest. Meanwhile, pretending not to be worried, she used medicines and poultices for her wound, and to help herself recover. She gave orders that Acceronia's will should be found and her goods placed under seal; this was the only thing she did openly.

Now Nero was waiting for the messengers to come and tell him that the crime had been carried out when word was brought that she had escaped only slightly wounded, but that after such risks there could be no doubt about who had caused it all. Scared half to death, Nero was sure that she would be there right away to get her revenge, either arming her slaves or stirring up the troops, or perhaps appealing to the Senate or to the masses, and blaming him for the wreck, her injury and the death of her friends. And what could he do against this to save his own skin? His chance for help lay with his advisers, Sextus Burrus and Seneca, whom he summoned at once; it is unclear whether or not they knew about the business in advance. Both men were silent for a long time, either because they were unwilling to argue with him, or because they really did believe that things had reached such a point that Agrippina had to be stopped, or Nero would be killed. After a while Seneca made a decision, looked at Burrus and asked whether the soldiers should be given the order to kill? Burrus answered that the Praetorians were under oath to the Julio-Claudian imperial family as a whole, that they revered the memory of Agrippina's father, Germanicus, and that they would not commit a crime against one of his children. He said that Anicetus should carry out what he had promised, and the latter asked right away for permission to do so. When he heard this, Nero said that he had been presented on that day with an empire, and that this great gift had been given him by a freedman. He told Anicetus to go at once, and take with him men who would obey orders without question. When Nero heard that Agermus had arrived with a message from Agrippina, he made him look guilty by planting a sword by his feet while he was delivering his message, and then having him put in chains, as if he had been caught in the act; he could then concoct a story of how his mother had plotted against his life, and, when detected, had committed suicide in shame.

Meanwhile, people had heard of the dangers that Agrippina had been in, but still thought that it had been an accident; when they heard, they rushed down to the beach, some climbed onto the sea-wall, some got hold of handy fishing-boats, and others waded waist-deep into the sea, some with their arms outstretched. All along the shore you could hear prayers, expressions of grief, all kinds of questions and unfounded answers. A huge crowd turned up, with torches, and when it became known that she had been rescued, they all set off to congratulate her, but were scattered by the sight of a threatening armed column of men. Anicetus put a cordon round her villa, broke down the door and arrested any slaves that appeared, until he reached her bedroom door. A few of her people were still there, but the rest had fled in terror at the invasion. In the dimly-lit bedroom there was only one single maid, and Agrippina was getting more and more worried that no word had come from her son, and that Agermus had not come back either. This all boded ill: the isolation, the sudden mayhem outside – all the signs of disaster. When the one maid tried to leave, Agrippina said, 'Are you deserting me as well?' and then she saw Anicetus, accompanied by Herculeius, a naval captain, and Obitarus, a centurion with the fleet. She told them that if Anicetus had come to visit her, he could report back that she was feeling better; if he had come with crime in mind, that she did not believe that any of this was her son's doing, because she would not sanction the killing of his mother. The assassins surrounded her bed, and the captain struck first, hitting her on the head with a club. As the centurion drew his sword to kill her, she pointed to her belly and shouted 'strike at the womb!' and was hacked and beaten to death.

Petronius

Died AD 65

Neronian courtier, satirist and poet

It is historically unproven but considered fairly certain that Titus Petronius, the most celebrated decadent figure of Nero's court after the emperor himself, was the author of the **Satyricon**, a picaresque novel set in Southern Italy containing the exploits of three homosexual adventurers. Much of what survives is fragmented but a manuscript emerged in seventeenth century Dalmatia containing in its entirety the chapter **Cena Trimalchionis** (Dinner at Trimalchio's) describing the banquet of a freed slave whose vast wealth is exceeded only by his vulgarity. Dinner at Trimalchio's is a masterpiece of comic observation and invention which it may be said captures the very spirit of the Roman world with wonderful vividness.

Petronius himself died following his implication in a famous conspiracy against Nero. Tacitus has left us a short account of his life and death which is itself worthy of inclusion in this volume.

TACITUS

from the *Annals*

XVI, 18–20: The Death of Petronius Arbiter

Petronius merits a few words to recall what he was like. He spent his days in sleep and his nights in official and social activities. Where others make it through hard work, Petronius got famous by being idle, but he was not thought of as a wastrel or as a dissolute, the way other layabouts are, but rather as a specialist in extravagant behaviour. His words and deeds were so unselfconsciously abandoned that they were freely accepted as 'refreshingly uncomplicated.' However, when he was proconsul and then consul at Bithynia in Asia Minor, he showed himself to be energetic, and well up to the job. But then he turned to a life of studied luxury – at least apparently so – and was admitted into Nero's close circle of intimates as his fashion consultant, his 'Arbiter of Elegance,' after which Nero pronounced nothing charming or fashionable unless it had Petronius' seal of approval. As a result, Tigellinus became envious of him, having found in him a rival who was more skilled in the arts of hedonism than he was. So Tigellinus exploited the emperor's cruel streak (which was Nero's predominant vice), and denounced Petronius on the grounds of his friendship with Scaevinus, bribing one of his slaves to turn informer, making sure no defence was possible, and arranging that most of Petronius' people were placed under arrest.

At that time Nero happened to be in the Campagna, and Petronius himself had reached Cumae before he was arrested. He refused to have anything to do with the hopes and fears associated with waiting. However, he did not rush to commit suicide. He cut his veins, but, as and when he felt like it he had them bound up or opened again; meanwhile he chatted with his friends, not on serious matters, or so that he would be famous for his great fortitude. He listened, not to expositions of the immortal soul or of the theory of knowledge, but to jolly songs and light verse. He gave some slaves presents and had a few of them whipped. He came to dinner and sat there in his half-dozing state, so that death (although it was forced on him) might *look* natural. In his will, too, he refused to behave like most similar compulsory suicides, and made no flattering noises about Nero, or Tigellinus, or some other important person. No, he wrote down all the emperor's vices, with the names of the dubious men or women that he had been to bed with, and went on to describe all aspects of the emperor's sexual inventiveness. He sealed the document and sent it to Nero, then broke his signet-ring so that no-one else could use it to endanger other people.

Nero wondered how details of his more original bedtime activities had got out, and he thought of Silia, who was a senator's wife, and therefore not unimportant. She had partnered him in all his lustful goings-on, and she was, moreover, a close friend of Petronius. For failing to keep quiet about what she had seen and done, she was exiled.

PETRONIUS ARBITER

from *The Satyricon*

Dinner at Trimalchio's *Satyricon*, 26–41

Now came the third day, and we were looking forward to a good feed, but we were so bruised and battered that flight seemed a better idea than recreation. And so we were making gloomy plans as to how to avoid the coming storm, when one of Agamemnon's slaves interrupted us as we stood there arguing and said, 'don't you know whose house the bash is at today? Trimalchio, a really well-heeled chap. He has a clock in his dining room, *and* a bugle-boy in uniform, to sound how much of his life has passed.' Therefore we carefully got dressed and forgot all the bad things that had happened, and then told Giton – who had up to now been attending us willingly – to follow us to the baths. When we got there, we began to stroll around in our fine togs, or rather to tell jokes and to circulate, when suddenly we saw an old man who was bald, wearing a reddish tunic and playing ball with some long-haired boys. It wasn't the boys that made us gape – though they were worth it; no, it was the old man, who was exercising, in his sandals, with a green ball. He never picked it up if it touched the ground, though. A slave had a leather bag full, and provided the players with them as needed. We also noticed a new twist to the game. Two eunuchs were standing at different points of the circle. One held a silver chamber-pot, and the other counted the balls – not those thrown quickly from hand to hand in the game, though, but those that fell to the ground. While we were staring in wonder at the brilliance of this show, Menelaus ran up and said, 'this is the man with whom you'll be dining, and in fact what you are now watching is the apéritif to the dinner.' Menelaus had just finished speaking when Trimalchio clicked his fingers. At this sign, one of the eunuchs came up and held out the chamber-pot as he played. His bladder relieved, Trimalchio called for water for his hands, splashed a little on his fingers, and then wiped them on the head of one of the boys.

It would take too long to pick out single incidents. We went into the baths, and once we were soaked with sweat we went straight into the cold room. Trimalchio, covered all over with oils, was being rubbed down, not with standard towels, but with a bath-robe of the softest wool. In front of him three masseurs were drinking Falernian wine, and because they were bickering, they spilt a fair amount. Trimalchio said that they were drinking his health. Wrapped in a scarlet cloak of wool, he was placed in a litter. Four runners covered in medals went in front of him, as did a little cart in which rode his favourite lad. The boy had an old man's face and bleary eyes, and was even uglier than his master, Trimalchio. A musician with a tiny set of pipes sat himself down by Trimalchio's head as he was carried off, and played for the whole journey as if whispering secrets into his ear.

We followed, by now full of admiration, and arrived at the same time as Agamemnon at the door, on which was stuck a placard with this written on it: *100 lashes for any slave leaving the house without his master's permission*. At the entrance stood the porter, dressed in green with a cherry-red belt, and he was shelling peas into a silver bowl. A magpie greeted visitors from a golden cage which hung above the doorway. While I was taking all of this in, I almost fell over backwards and broke my leg. For on the left hand side as you went in, not far from the porter's lodge, was a massive dog on a chain – painted on the wall, and above it in block capitals was *CAVE CANEM – Beware of the Dog*! My companions laughed at me, but I plucked up my courage, and went to look at the whole wall. There was a fresco of a slave market, with everything labelled. Trimalchio was there with long hair, holding the staff of Mercury, while Minerva was leading him into Rome. The artist had painstakingly depicted his whole career with explanations underneath – how he had learnt accountancy and finally been made treasurer. Where the colonnade ended, Mercury held him by his chin and carried him up to a lofty platform for magistrates. The goddess Fortune stood before him with her overflowing horn of plenty, and the three Fates spinning their golden threads were there as well. I also noticed a group of sprinters exercising with their trainer by the colonnade. I spied, too, a large cupboard in the corner in which was a little shrine with the silver household gods, a marble statue of Venus, and large golden casket in which they said the clippings were kept from the first time Trimalchio had shaved.

I began to ask the porter what pictures they had in the central part of the house. 'The *Iliad* and the *Odyssey*,' he said. 'And the gladiatorial games put on by Laenas.' I couldn't take it all in.

Now we went through to the dining room. At the entrance sat the treasurer, going through the accounts. I was particularly surprised to see the ceremonial fasces and axes fixed onto the frame of the dining room door, one part of which was finished off as a kind of bronze ship's prow, inscribed *To Gaius Pompeius Trimalchio, Priest of the College of Augustus, from his Steward Cinnamus*. A double lamp hung from the ceiling underneath this inscription, and two little noticeboards were fastened onto each doorpost, one of which had, if I remember correctly, the words *Note: On December 30 and 31, Trimalchio will not be dining at home*. The other was painted with the course of the moon and representations of the sun and planets. Lucky and unlucky days were marked with various types of studs.

Having had our fill of these delights, we tried to get into the dining room, but one of the boys (who had this as his appointed task) shouted, 'right foot first!' Of course we were worried for a second, in case one of us had crossed the threshold contrary to the rule. As we were all stepping forward, right feet first, a stripped slave fell at our feet and started to beg us to save him from a beating. He wasn't in trouble for anything very serious – the steward's clothes had been stolen from him at the baths, and those clothes were hardly worth ten sesterces anyway. So we withdrew our right feet and begged the steward, who was counting gold pieces in the hall, to let the slave off. He looked up superciliously and said, 'the actual *loss* doesn't bother me, it's just this lazy wretch's carelessness. He lost my dinner clothes, and a client gave them to me for my birthday. Absolutely genuine Tyrian purple. But it had been washed once. Still, what can you do? He's all yours.'

We were much obliged for this great benevolence, and when we went into the dining room, the slave for whom we had pleaded ran up to us and to our great surprise waylaid us and showered us with kisses and thanked us for our kindness. 'Above all, you will know in a second who it is you have done the favour for. The master's wine is the waiter's to present.'

At last we sat down, and Alexandrian boys poured water cooled with snow over our hands. Others followed them in, and, squatting at our feet cut our toenails with great skill. Even such an unpleasant duty as this one didn't shut them up, and they kept on singing as they worked. I wanted to find out if the whole household sang, so I asked for a drink. A boy at hand got me one, singing away shrilly, and anyone asked to do something did the same. It was more like a music hall than a formal dinner.

Some rich and tasty starters were now brought on, as everyone had sat down except for Trimalchio, who, following the new custom, kept the head of the table for himself. A donkey made of Corinthian bronze was standing ready, and in its two panniers there were white olives on one side and black on the other. The donkey was hidden by two silver dishes, around the perimeters of each was inscribed the name *Trimalchio*, and the weight of each. Little iron trivets on the dishes supported dormice in honey and poppy seed. Then there were hot sausages on a silver griddle with damsons and pomegranate seeds underneath to represent coals. While we were eating these hors d'oeuvres, Trimalchio was brought in to musical accompaniment, and placed amongst a pile of little pillows. Those not expecting this laughed. His cropped head stuck out of his scarlet robe, and around his neck there was a cravat with a wide purple stripe, fringed with tassels. On the pinkie of his left hand he had a heavy gold-plated ring, and on the last joint of his ring finger was a smaller one that seemed to me to be solid gold, but in reality was set with little iron stars. Showing off even more wealth, he had bared his right arm, round which was a gold bracelet and an ivory bangle fastened with a bright metal clasp. Then, picking his teeth with a silver toothpick, he said, 'friends, I wasn't ready to come into the dining room yet, but I would have held you back had I delayed any longer. I have given up my own pleasures for your benefit. Allow me, though, to finish off my game.' A boy followed him with a board made from terebinth wood, with crystal squares, and then I noticed the most beautiful thing of all. He had gold and silver coins instead of black and white counters. While he played, Trimalchio kept up a running commentary, and we were still on the starters when a tray with a basket on it was brought in. In it was a wooden hen with her wings spread around, as they are when they are hatching. Two slaves came up at once and the music rose to a crescendo as they began to search through the straw, from which they produced peacock's eggs and handed them round to the guests. Trimalchio turned and looked at this scene and said, 'friends, I ordered that peacock's eggs be placed under an ordinary chicken. My word – I hope that they are not going to hatch! Let's try, though, and see if you can still suck them.' We took our spoons – they weighed at least half a pound each – and cracked our pastry-cased eggs. I almost threw my share away, for it looked as though the chicken was already formed. Then I heard a regular guest of Trimalchio's say, 'I wonder what treat we have here.' I poked through the shell with a finger and found a little fat *beccafico*, covered in seasoned egg yolk.

By now Trimalchio, breaking off his game, asked in a loud voice for all the dishes to be brought to him, and asked whether any of us wished to take a second glass of wine sweetened with honey. Suddenly the music gave a sign, and the hors d'oeuvres were whipped away by a group of singing slaves. In the muddle, a small silver dish happened to fall on the floor and a boy picked it up. Trimalchio noticed this accident and ordered him to thrown down the dish again. A cleaner came in and began to sweep up this silver with other rubbish. Two long-haired Ethiopians with little wine-skins came in, just like sprinklers in the amphitheatre, and poured wine over our hands – for no one offered us water.

The host was praised for his most extravagant arrange-ments. 'Mars loves a fair fight,' he said, 'and for that reason I ordered everyone be shown to a separate table. In this way the smelly slaves won't make us so hot as they push past us.'

Glass amphorae, carefully corked with gypsum were then brought in. Around their necks were fixed labels which said: *Vintage Falernian, Bottled in the Praetorship of Opimius, 100 years old*. While we were studying the labels, Trimalchio clapped his hands and said, 'well, wine lives longer than poor old mankind. Let's have a ball! Wine is life. I'm giving you a real vintage – last century, no less! I didn't serve such good stuff at dinner yesterday, and the guests were a much better class of person.'

And so we drank and admired all the trappings. A slave brought in a silver skeleton, made so that its limbs and spine could be moved and bent in all directions. He put it down on the table a couple of times, setting its flexible joints to strike various poses, and Trimalchio declaimed:

> Look! Man is just a bag of bones
> He's here, and gone tomorrow!
> We'll soon be like this fellow, so
> let's live! Let's drown our sorrow!

After the applause a platter followed, not as big as expected, but so novel that everyone stared. It was a round platter with the twelve signs of the zodiac on it and above each the master-chef had placed some special food suitable to the attributes of the sign. Above Aries, a ramekin of buttered chickpeas; above Taurus, a steak; above Gemini, testicles and kidneys; above Cancer, a garland; above Leo, an African fig; above Virgo, a young sow's udder; above Libra, a pair of scales with a tart on one side and a cake on the other; above Scorpio, a little sea-fish; above Sagittarius, a bullseye; above Capricorn, a lobster; above Aquarius, a goose; and above Pisces, two mullets. In the centre was a honeycomb on a clump of grass.

An Egyptian boy brought bread round in a silver dish, murdering as he did so a hit from a recent musical in an incredibly offensive voice. We sat down rather miserably at such cut-price food. 'I recommend that we eat,' said Trimalchio. 'This is the real sauce of our dinner.' As he said this, four dancers pranced up in time to the music and removed the top half of the dish. Inside it we then saw corn-fed fowls, sows' udders and a hare in the middle. It had wings attached to look like Pegasus. In the corners we spotted four figures of the satyr Marsyas, and from their wine-skins a peppery sauce flowed out over the fishes, who seemed to swim in a rivulet. Started off by the household, we all applauded this, and set off on these trifles with a laugh. Trimalchio was as pleased as we were with the trickery he had played, and called out 'Carve 'em!' A man came up immediately and in time to music he carved up the meat in such a way that you would have thought he was a gladiator, fencing to musical accompaniment. In a very soft voice Trimalchio carried on saying "Carve 'em, Carve 'em!' I suspected that this repetition was part of a joke, and I wasn't ashamed to ask the man sitting next to me. He had watched this game more often than I had, and explained, 'you see that man slicing up the meat? – his name is Carveham. So whenever Trimalchio says "carve 'em," he's calling out the name and the order.'

I wasn't able to eat much more, so I turned to my

dinner companion to find out as much as possible – I started to dig for gossip, and to find out who the woman was who was running about all over the place. 'She's called Fortunata. She's Trimalchio's wife, and she counts her money by the roomful. And before she married him, what was she? I would not have taken a piece of bread – pardon my French – from her poxy hand. No-one knows how or why, but now she's in seventh heaven and is Trimalchio's reason for living. In fact, if she were to tell him that it was dark at midday, he'd believe it. He doesn't even know how much he has, he's that rich. But this vixen keeps an eye on everything, even where you wouldn't think she could. She's cold, sober and sharp as a knife, but she's got a wicked tongue and jolly well uses it. If she likes you, she likes you; if she doesn't, she doesn't. Trimalchio has estates it would take a hawk a day to fly over. The man is worth millions. There is more silver lying around in his porter's lodge than others have in their entire bank-accounts. And have you seen his household? Ye gods! I really don't believe that one in ten knows their own master by sight. He could blow any of your young upstarts right out of the water. And don't think that he buys anything, either. Everything is grown at home – wool, lemons, pepper. You could have hen's milk if you wanted. At one time his wool wasn't of a good enough quality, so he bought Tarentine rams and crossbred them in with his flock. He ordered bees from Athens so that he could have Attic honey at home (and, by the way, his own bees were improved by the little Greek fellows). Look, within the last couple of days he has written off to India for some mushroom spores. And he doesn't have a single mule which wasn't fathered by a wild ass. You see all of these cushions? Every one of them has either purple or crimson stuffing. That's true happiness. Make sure you don't look down on the other freedmen here. They're loaded. You see that one reclining on the very bottom couch? Today he's worth a good eight hundred K. It grew from nothing. A little time ago he was carrying wood on his back. I don't know, but they do say that he found a pot of gold at the end of the rainbow. Still, I'm not jealous of what the gods give. Anyway, he can still remember the feel of his master's slap, and he wants to indulge himself. And so he has just put up a notice on the dump where he lives, saying *Gaius Pompeius Diogenes – Attic to let from July 1. Owner has recently purchased house.* And then that one there, in the freedman's place. How well he's had it! I don't blame him. He had a million, but he invested badly. Now I don't think he can call his hair his own. But I'd swear it wasn't his fault, and there isn't a better chap alive, but his own bloody freedmen took him for everything. You know how it is – your company's pot goes off the boil and when things start to go downhill, your friends disappear. You see him like this, but what a responsible business he used to run! He was an undertaker. He used to eat meals fit for a king – whole roast boar, wonderful pastry creations and game – he kept cooks and pastry-chefs. There was more wine spilt under his table than others have in their cellars. He lived in a dream more than in reality. When he was scared that his creditors would think that he might have to file for bankruptcy, when things were going badly, he advertised a sale: *Gaius Julius Proculus will be auctioning off a few surplus knick-knacks.*'

Trimalchio interrupted this wonderful flow of reminiscences. The course had now been taken away and the mellowing guests began to pay attention to the wine and the general conversation, when he lay back on his couch and said, 'you must make this wine slip down pleasantly. Fish need to swim. I ask you, did you really think I would be happy with that course? The one you saw on the other part of the dish? "Is this," as Vergil put it, "the Ulysses we know and love?" Well, is it? We must have culture, even at dinner. God rest the bones of my patron, he wanted me to be a real gentleman among gentlemen. No one can teach *me* anything new, as that last dish proved. Heaven, where the twelve gods live, changes into that number of shapes. First it becomes Aries the ram, and whoever is born under that sign has many flocks, a lot of wool, a hard head, a lot of front, and sharp horns. Many academics are born under that sign, as well as woolly-minded people.' We applauded the panache of our astrologer, and so he continued, 'then the whole sky becomes a little bull. People who run at things like a bull at a gate are born then, as well as cowboys and cud-chewers. Under Gemini, however, you get pairs-in-hand, yoked oxen, men with big balls, and people who sit on the fence. I was born under Cancer, so I stand on my own feet and own a lot of property on land and at sea – because a crab is as happy on both. That's why I didn't put anything above Cancer earlier, in case I weighed down my own horoscope. Greedy and tyrannical people are born under Leo; under Virgo, women, fugitives and members of chain-gang; under Libra, butchers, perfume makers and anyone who weighs things up first; under Scorpio, poisoners and hit-men; cross-eyed people are born under Sagittarius, the ones who look at the two veg., but take the meat; under Capricorn you get poor beggars whose bad luck makes them grow horns; under Aquarius, publicans and drips; under Pisces, fish-chefs and political piss-artists. So the world turns like a mill-wheel, and there is always trouble. Men being born or dying. You saw the turf in the middle of the platter with a honey comb on it? I do everything for a reason. Mother Earth is in the middle, round like an egg, and she has all the goodness inside her, just like a honeycomb.

'Genius,' we all exclaimed, raising our hands to the ceiling and swearing that even Hipparchus and Aratus – the greatest Greek astronomers – could not compare with Trimalchio. Then the servants came up and spread covers on the couches, embroidered with nets, hunters with hunting spears and all the accoutrements that go with hunting. We still didn't know what to look at first, when there was a huge rumpus just outside the dining room. Spartan hunting dogs began to run all over the place – even round the table. Close on their tails came a huge platter with a wild boar of immense size on it. It was wearing a freedman's cap, and two baskets made of palm leaves hung from its tusks. One was full of the best fresh dates and the other full of the best dried dates. Around it were little piglets made of cake, placed as if they were suckling, and thus suggesting that it was a sow. These were in fact presents to take away. Surprisingly the man who came to divide up the boar was not old Carveham, who'd cut up the game, but a huge bearded man, wearing leggings and a damask hunting-coat. He pulled out a hunting knife and stabbed it hard into the boar's side and out from it flew a flock of thrushes. But there were bird catchers ready with limed twigs as snares, and as the birds flew round the dining room they caught them in a moment. Trimalchio ordered that each guest be presented with a bird and then said, 'now look at all the acorns this woodland boar has eaten.' At once boys went to the baskets which dangled from the tusks and divided up the dried and fresh dates equally among the guests.

In the meantime, I had kept quiet, because I was trying out to myself all sorts of ideas as to why the boar had come in with a freedman's cap on. After I had come up with all kinds of dumb answers, I asked my knowledgeable neighbour what was bothering me. He said, 'even your slave could explain that to you. There's no mystery. It's perfectly obvious. This boar was brought in yesterday as a last course, but he was let go by the guests. So today he comes back to dinner as a free man.' I cursed my slowness, and didn't ask any more questions in case it looked as if I had never dined in company before.

Suetonius

The Fire of Rome

The phrase 'Nero fiddled while Rome burned' is of course
anachronistic, since there were no 'fiddles' in Nero's time.
It might however serve as an apposite metaphor for the
fact that Nero was not interested in the business of government, and abandoned himself – to the scandal of the Roman
people – to his passion for performing music and drama
upon the public stage, while his corrupt ministers and
agents were allowed to despoil the empire. It is generally
agreed among modern historians that Nero was not responsible for the great fire that ravaged Rome in AD 64. Indeed
he was not in Rome at the time but staying in Antium on
the Latium coast, and he hurried back when news was
brought, to organise efforts to fight the blaze.

It is agreed by ancient historians, however, that he did
sing, while the fire raged, his composition 'The Fall of
Troy' while accompanying himself on the lyre. It is quite
likely to be true. The sheer epic drama of the situation may
have been more than he could resist. Some ancient sources,
Suetonius included, accuse him directly of having started
the fire, and his subsequent act of claiming a large area of
the ruined city centre to build his vast new palace complex,
the Domus Aurea or Golden House – the ultimate gentleman's folly – doubtless made the whole tragedy seem suspicious to his contemporaries.

Nero showed no mercy to the people, nor to the walls of his capital city. In general conversation someone once said to him, 'when I am dead, let fire consume the earth.' Nero retorted, 'no, rather while I am still alive.' And he meant it, too. As if disgusted by the ugliness of the old buildings and the narrow, winding streets, he set fire to the city of Rome so openly that although a number of high-ranking public officials caught the emperor's men with dry flax and wood on their estates, they did not do anything to stop them. There were some storehouses on land near the palace, his Golden House, land which he greatly desired. Because their walls were made of stone, these storehouses were destroyed with machines of war and then burnt to the ground. Destruction raged for six days and seven nights – so much so that the people of Rome were forced to find shelter in public monuments and tombs. During the fire, the houses of former military leaders – still decorated with the spoils of war – and temples of the gods, dedicated either by the kings, or later, in the Punic and Gallic wars, were also burned, as were a great number of blocks of flats. So, too, was anything else worth seeing and notable that had survived from ancient times. Looking down at this blaze from the tower of Maecenas and revelling in what he called, 'the beauty of the flames,' he chanted the 'Lay of the Fall of Troy,' wearing his usual stage clothes. To get as much booty and riches as possible from this, he promised the free removal of corpses and rubble, but did not allow anyone to get near what remained of his property. From the donations that he not only received, but also actually demanded, he almost bankrupted the provinces and people.

Tacitus

The Banquet of Tigellinus

An account of what would seem to be a fairly typical
Neronian orgy.

XV, 37: A TYPICAL
NERONIAN ORGY

Nero, wishing to make it look as if nowhere pleased him
as much as Rome, began to give banquets in public places
there, and indeed to use the whole city as if it were his
house. The most celebrated and extravagant feast was that
given by Tigellinus, and I shall describe it as a typical
example, to save myself from repeating over and over
again the same tale of wanton behaviour. He had a great
raft built on the Lake of Agrippa, and on that he held the
banquet, while other vessels pulled it along. These other
ships were decorated with gold and ivory, and the rowers
were all perverts, arranged according to age and special
sexual skills. He had also collected wild animals and birds
and sea-beasts from every corner of the earth and from
the ocean. On the shores of the lake were brothels, stocked
with high-born ladies, and nearby you could see completely naked whores. First there were obscene dances and
gestures, and then, when it got dark, songs and bright
lights became audible and visible in all the woods and
houses nearby. Nero had already become totally familiar
with every kind of lust, natural or unnatural, and left no
vice untried that would make him even more corrupt than
he already was – except that a few days after this feast he
'married' (and with full ceremonial!) one of the mob of
perverts, a man called Pythagoras. The emperor wore a
bridal veil and there were witnesses, a dowry, a marriage
bed and ceremonial torches. Everything was on show
which is normally covered by night, even when the bride
is actually a woman.

Martial

AD 40–104

Epigrammatist

Marcus Valerius Martialis was born in Spain and went to
live in Rome in AD 64. His literary talents won him
numerous wealthy and influential acquaintances and pa-
trons, including the emperors Titus and Domitian, and a
number of honours and privileges were granted him, but
his situation remained financially precarious, choosing as he
did to live solely by his pen. His short, witty poems
concentrated upon the human weaknesses he saw about
him in Roman life, yet are ultimately good natured and
lack the real malice and bitterness so conspicuous in the
satires of his contemporary and friend Juvenal.

MARTIAL

from the *Epigrams*

I, 34

You always do it with the doors wide open, Lesbia!
Why ever don't you fornicate more secretly?
You seem to like spectators more than lovers. Why?
Don't you *enjoy* it, when there's no-one there to see?

At least a whore will operate behind the drapes.
Go to the brothel – you won't find a spy-hole there,
ask any of the girls! And even for a stand-
up job they'll hide behind the statue of the mayor.

In case it seems I'm being far too hard on you,
it's getting *caught* – not screwing – I'm objecting to.

II, 82

Why did you cut the tongue out of that slave before
you had him crucified, Ponticus? How could you ignore
that though he's silent, folk talk all the more?

III, 12

Fabullus, I grant last night you gave
your dinner-guests some splendid aftershave,
– but nothing they could chew!
                There's something new!
'Perfumed but ravenous,' anointed but unfed?
Both look to me a little bit like being dead.

VII, 35

Rotten wife and rotten husband! I can tell
their lifestyles match in every way as well.
It's just . . . I wonder why they fight like hell?

VII, 43

Fabius buries all his wives. Chrestilla sees to
husbands. The marriage-bed has been a pyre a few
times now.
Venus, unite them! Send this triumphant two
to learn at *first* hand what the undertakers do.

IX, 33

If from some changing-room rounds of applause you
hear I bet it's Maro's massive cock that's raised a cheer!

X. 97

The pyre was laid out neatly, ready to be fired,
we stood there with the incense, by his weeping wife,
the bier and tomb were bought, the undertaker hired,
and *I* was in the will!
Then he came back to life.

XI, 56

Stoic Chaeremon, how you sing of 'welcome death!'
Surely you don't expect that I would waste my breath
on praise for *that*? Your stoic airs and graces
come from tatty crockery and empty fire-places,
torn carpets, lice, or sleeping on a rock-hard bed,
still in some short-arsed toga worn down to a thread!
Oh, what a noble chap is he, who can ignore
his lack of lousy wine, black bread and bedding-straw!

Now if your bed had purple blankets, full and fluffed,
and if your pillows with merino wool were stuffed,
and tucked in with you was the boy who served the wine,
(the pretty red–lipped lad the guests thought rather fine),
oh, then you'd want to live three times as long on earth
as old Methuselah, not lose a minute's worth!

Condemning life is easy when the good time's gone.
The hard part, when you're wretched, is to carry on.

XI, 62

Lesbia swears she's never in her whole life fucked for free.
It's true! When she wants fucking, she will always pay the
fee.

Josephus

Born AD 37

Jewish Historian

Following the eventual overthrow and suicide of Nero (AD 68) and the assassination of his unpopular successor Galba (AD 69) the empire was plunged into a brutal civil war between three rival claimants to the throne. The eventual victor was Vespasian, founder of the Flavian dynasty. He had been appointed by Nero as commander of the Roman forces in Judaea, to quell the Jewish revolt of AD 66–70. Josephus served in the war as a Jewish commander in the siege of Jotapata. Captured by the Romans, he was brought before Vespasian, whose favour he won, reputedly by prophesying his imperial destiny. Later, under Vespasian's protection, he went to live in Rome, where he wrote his history of the Jewish War, losing no opportunity in the process to justify his own often less than honourable behaviour.

Having made his grip upon the empire secure, Vespasian dispatched his son Titus to complete the subjugation of the Jews. The following is Josephus' depiction of Vespasian's and Titus' Triumph – the thanksgiving procession of a military commander and his victorious army through the streets of Rome – following their reconquest of rebel Judaea.

JOSEPHUS

The Triumph of Vespasian

From *The Jewish Wars*, VII, 123–50 (VII, 4–7)

The soldiers had marched out in centuries and cohorts under their commanders while it was still dark, and were drawn up not near the gates of the Upper Palace on the Palatine Hill, but near to the Temple of Isis on the Campus Martius. The generals had spent the night there, and at dawn Vespasian and Titus came out wearing laurel wreaths and the traditional purple robes, and went to the Portico of Octavia. There the full Senate, the chief magistrates, and the order of knights were all waiting for them. A daïs with ivory chairs on it for them had been set up in front of the colonnade, and they sat down, whereupon the soldiers at once started shouting out with delight, and acclaiming their bravery with a single voice. They themselves were unarmed, wearing silk robes and laurels. After he had acknowledged the cheers of the soldiers, Vespasian gave a sign for silence, even though they wanted to go on for longer. A complete silence descended, and the emperor got up, covered most of his head with his cloak and offered up the usual prayers. Titus did the same thing. Vespasian made a brief speech to the assembled group after the prayers, and then dismissed the soldiers to the meal that victorious generals usually gave. Vespasian himself withdrew to the Gate of triumph – so-called because the triumphal processions pass through it. There, he and Titus broke their own fast, and then put on the triumphal garments and made sacrifices to the gods whose images are on each side of the gate. After that they continued the triumphal procession, moving through the various theatres on the way, so that the crowds would get a better view.

It would not be possible to do justice to the many sights that were to be seen – works of art, displays of riches, natural wonders. Almost all the treasures that fortune-favoured men have ever got their hands on – the fantastic riches of many nations – were brought together that day and it all bore witness to the greatness of the Roman Empire. Vast amounts of silver, gold and ivory in every shape imaginable was on display, but not as if they were being carried in a triumphal procession – rather as if it were some flowing river. Tapestries were carried along, some in the rarest purple, and others with life portraits by Babylonian artists; clear gemstones, some set in golden crowns, and some differently set, were carried past in such huge numbers that it made us rethink our notions that any of them were actually rare at all. Then came massive and beautifully crafted images of the gods, every one made from expensive materials. Many species of animal were led past, all adorned with the proper trappings. Each group of beasts was accompanied by a large group of men dressed in clothes which were dyed with genuine Tyrian purple and which had gold thread woven in. These attendants, hand-picked for the triumphal procession, all wore marvellous and unbelievably expensive ornaments. Not even the rabble of captives were unadorned. The variety and beauty of their clothes hid any ugliness caused by physical suffering. But nothing in the triumph caused as much excitement as the floats, the tall-structured pageant-wagons. In fact, their size caused concern, as people worried about their stability. Many were three or four stories high, and their magnificent trappings were a source of delight as well as surprise. Many were hung with tapestries interwoven with gold thread, which all had ivory and gold frames. There were various tableaux showing successive stages in the war, depicting the people and the events very vividly. One picture showed a prosperous country being laid waste; another showed whole enemy battalions being massacred; men running away and men being taken prisoner; huge walls being smashed by siege-engines and fortresses being attacked; cities with good defences completely overrun, with the Roman army pouring across their ramparts; a sea of blood, with those unable to resist raising their hands in surrender; temples set on fire and homes pulled down about their owners' heads; and after complete desolation and misery the river flowing not through cultivated fields, or supplying water to man and beast, but through a country still engulfed in flames. These were the sufferings that the Jews had to undergo when they set out upon this war. The artistry and great craftsmanship of these pageant-displays showed the events to those who had not experienced them as if they were happening before their very eyes. On each float was the leader of a captured city, posed in the position in which he had been taken prisoner. Following these pageant-wagons, a number of ships were carried along, too. Most of the plunder was piled up haphazardly, but more prominent than the rest was the treasure taken at the Temple in Jerusalem: a golden table weighing many talents of bullion, and a gold *menorah*, a candelabra made differently from the ones we usually use. There was a central shaft fitted onto a base, and from it extended thin branches, a bit like a trident, and at the end of each branch was a lamp. There were seven of these, representing the great significance given to that number by Jews. A set of *Torah*-scrolls, the Jewish Law, was carried after this and all the other treasures. Next came a large group of men carrying images of Victory herself, made out of gold or ivory, and behind them rode Vespasian and then Titus. Domitian rode beside them, dressed magnificently, on a finely caparisoned horse.

The triumph ended at the temple of Capitoline Jove, where the procession halted. It was an ancient custom to wait there until news came that the enemy general had been executed. The general involved was Simon, son of Gioras, who had walked in the procession with the prisoners-of-war. Now, with a noose thrown round his neck, he was dragged to the usual place in the Forum, while his guards beat him. Roman Law specifies that those condemned to death as enemies of the state should be executed at that spot. The news of his death was greeted with universal shouting, and the sacrifices were begun. After the imperial family had made the customary and appropriate prayers, they returned to the palace. Some people were entertained at their table, while great banquets had been arranged for the others in their own homes. Rome celebrated all day the victorious campaign against its enemies, the end of civil disturbances, and the hope for future successes.

When the triumphal ceremonies were over and the Roman Empire most firmly established, Vespasian decided to build a temple to Peace. This was surprisingly quickly finished, and artistically it went beyond all human imagination. Apart from the fact that he had unlimited wealth available, Vespasian also decorated it with ancient masterpieces of paintings and statues. In fact, objects that men had wandered all over the world to see, eager to set eyes on them when they were in different countries, were now collected and placed in this temple. Here, too, he placed the golden ritual vessels (he gloried in having taken these) from the Temple of Jerusalem. The Laws, and the purple hangings from the Holy of Holies, however, he ordered to be placed in his palace.

AN ADVENTURE IN THE EAST

Satyricon, 85–7

When I was in the eastern part of the empire, working for a treasury official, I stayed at a house in Pergamum. I stayed there willingly, not just because of the elegant house, but also because of my host's incredibly handsome son. I had thought out a plan how to become his lover without his father realising, and whenever at dinner the subject was brought up of taking advantage of good-looking boys, I flew into a complete rage and said so sternly that my ears were offended by these dirty stories that the mother, especially, looked on me favourably as a philosopher. After that I began to take the youth to the gymnasium, to arrange his schooling, to teach him, and in anticipation of my own intentions, to warn his parents not to let any potential seducers into the house . . .

One day, when a public holiday had cut short our work, we were resting in the dining room, too lazy to go to bed because of our prolonged partying. Around midnight I noticed that the boy was still awake. So in a very quiet whisper I prayed: 'Mistress Venus, if I could kiss this boy without him noticing, I would give him a pair of doves tomorrow.'

The boy began to snore when he heard the cost of my pleasure, so I snuck up to the little impostor and fell upon him with kisses. Happy with this beginning I got up early the next morning and brought him the pair of doves he was waiting for, and so fulfilled my promise. The next night I had another chance, but this time I changed my prayer and said, 'If I can run my lustful hands all over him without him feeling anything, I will give him two of the very fiercest fighting cocks for it.' Hearing this prayer, the boy himself moved over to me and, I think, began to get worried that *I* might fall asleep. Of course, I gave him no grounds for concern, and so I gorged myself on his whole body without the ultimate pleasure. When day came, I brought the happy boy what I had promised.

On the third night, I had another opportunity. I got up and murmured into the ear of the boy, who was apparently sleeping rather badly: 'Immortal gods, if you allow him to sleep and let me have my full desires and full intercourse, for this pleasure I will give the boy the best Macedonian thoroughbred horse. The one condition is that he notice nothing.' The youth had never slept so soundly. First of all, I ran my hands over his milk-white breast, soon I was stuck to his lips, and finally all my desires came to a single head. The next morning he sat in his room and waited for me to follow my usual routine. Well, you know how much easier it is to buy doves and fighting cocks than thoroughbred horses, and anyway, I was scared in case a present that was so far over the top might make my generosity a bit suspect. After I had wandered around for a few hours, when I came back to the house I only gave the boy a kiss. He looked about as he threw his arms about my neck and asked, 'Please sir, where's my horse.'

Breaking my word had effectively denied me access, but I returned to my licentious ways. A few days later, a similar chance left us in the same position. When I heard the father snoring, I began to ask the youth to let us become friends again, and to let himself be satisfied by my love, and all the other things that you say out of rampant desire. He was clearly angry and only said, 'Go to sleep or I'll tell my father on you.' Nothing is impossible, however, if you are really prepared to be depraved. Even as he said, 'I'll wake father,' I crawled into bed with him and took my pleasure despite his (faint) resistance. In actual fact, he was not unpleased with my naughtiness. After a long complaint about how he had been deceived, made fun of and bitched about by his classmates because he had boasted about my wealth, he said, 'you'll see that I'm not as mean as you. Do it again if you want.'

I was back in favour with the boy, all of his hard feelings gone, and after abusing his kindness I went to sleep. The boy was not happy with just one encore, because he was fully developed and of an age where he was eager for more. So he woke me from my sleep and said, 'Don't you want anything?' Of course it wasn't that much of a chore. Therefore, though I was shattered by all the sweating and grunting, he got what he wanted, and I fell asleep again, exhausted by pleasure. Less than an hour later he began to poke me and said, 'why aren't we doing it?' Then I completely lost my temper at being woken up so often, and I used his own words back at him, 'go to sleep or *I'll* tell your father on *you*.'

Cassius Dio

Born AD 163/4

Roman Historian

Cassius Dio was a distinguished senator and a friend and colleague to numerous emperors. He wrote a complete history of Rome from its foundation to the death of the emperor Alexander Severus in AD 235, and is a major source of information for the events of the second and early third centuries, to many of which he was a first hand witness. His straightforward and often curiously naive approach is a far cry from the subtle complexities of Tacitus, but much of the information he conveys is unique and invaluable.

The following extract describes an event in the reign of Domitian, the second son of Vespasian and last emperor of the Flavian dynasty, who ruled from 81–96 AD following the early death of his brother Titus. Domitian was a grim and suspicious man much feared and hated by the senate – understandably, given this bizarre story of Dio's.

CASSIUS DIO

from *The Roman History*

LXVII, 9

On that occasion, then, Domitian provided delights for the
masses; but on another occasion he entertained the senior
senators and members of the nobility like this – he had a
room prepared that was black everywhere, on the ceiling,
the walls and the floor, with plain couches of the same
colour on the bare floorboards. Then he invited the guests
in singly, at night, and unattended. And first he put beside
each one a *stele*, a grave-tablet with the guest's own
name, and a little lamp of the sort placed in tombs. Then
in came some pretty boys, naked and painted black, like
phantoms, who moved around in a frightening dance, and
then one stood at the feet of each guest. And after this,
things that are normally offered at sacrifices for the dead,
all black, and on dishes of the same colour, were set out, so
that every guest was trembling with fear, all of them
expecting their throats to be cut. This was made worse by
the fact that everyone there kept completely silent, as if
they were already in the halls of the dead, except for
Domitian, who only talked about death and killing. In the
end he dismissed them all, but he had already sent away
their own slaves (who had been waiting in the hall) and
now handed them over to ones they did not know, to be
taken off in coaches or litters. This filled their minds with
much greater anxiety. And just as each guest reached his
home and had begun to breathe again, he was told that
there was a message from Domitian Augustus. This time,
while they were waiting to die, someone brought in the
guest's *stele* (which was made of silver), and then gradually
others brought in different things, including the dinner
dishes, which were very expensively made. And at the end
came the boy who had been the 'ghost' of each guest, now

cleaned and adorned. So after having been terrified for an entire night, the guests now received their gifts.

Juvenal

Born AD 55?

Satirist

Little is known for certain about the life of Decimus Junius Juvenalis. He was probably the son of a wealthy Spanish ex-slave, who embarked upon a successful public career, but was supposedly exiled to Egypt by Domitian for some offence given in his writings. He was recalled to Rome after Domitian's assassination in AD 96, his wealth, position and career lost and, forced to live in humiliating circumstances, produced a series of marvellous and vitriolic satires which parade the warts of the Roman scene before us with unrivalled vividness.

JUVENAL

from the *Satires*

III

It makes me want to run off to the German woods,
or to the Arctic, when the Hooray-Henrys dare
to talk of morals, when they live such drunken lives!
First, they know nothing, even though they always own
a bust of Aristotle or some other great,
have miniatures of famous stoics on their shelves.
Don't trust a face! In every back-street you can find
some solemn-featured lush.

       Do *you* perhaps complain
of falling moral standards, while you act the fag
for all the smart set? Yes, your hairy chest and arms
bespeak a manly soul; and yet your bum is smooth,
and doctors snigger archly when they treat your piles.

Such men look strong and taciturn, the silent type,
they keep their crewcuts shorter than their eyebrows, but
I'd rather have an old queen any day! At least
he's honest. You can see his nature (blame his genes!),
his obviousness needs pity, camp behaviour is
its own excuse. Far worse are those who shout
and moralise in macho language about vice,
whilst peddling arse! 'Respect *you*, ducky? You're as camp
as me! How am I worse than you,' says our old queen.
Straight-limbed lads mock cripples and white men sneer
at blacks.
But would you like conspirators to criticise
a putsch? You'd think the world had turned right
upside-down if gangsters all bewailed the rise of robbery-
with-violence, or ancient lechers railed against
adultery, or despots claimed purges were bad!

Domitian, an adulterer in the classic mould,
had just revived tough laws on sex that scared them all
(yes, even Mars and Venus!), when young Julia,
his fecund niece, had four aborted babies, all
of which resembled her Imperial Uncle. Surely
every miserable sinner should despise such
moral hypocrites, and throw their censure back at
them.

One sour old matron always used to rabbit on:
'What happened to our good old marriage-laws?'
Miss X, a prostitute, soon had enough, and laughed, and
said: 'Hurrah! A moral guardian! Rome has regained
a sense of shame. The puritans are back! But isn't
that 'Seduction' perfuming your hairy neck?
Where did you get it? Tell me, come, don't be ashamed!

If you're concerned about old-fashioned laws, though,
what about the one on buggery? Just have a look at what
men do! They're far worse than us, but there are
more of them. Besides, they hide behind male-bonding!
Nancy-boys all stick together, but you'll never find
amongst us women such perverted goings-on.
Mary won't use her tongue on Jane, nor Jill on Sue,
but Harry likes it both ways round with his young
men.

Do we plead in the courts? Nit-pick legalities?
Bluster before the bench? There really aren't too
many lady wrestlers either (too much red meat!).
You spin your wool well, and then bring it back again
in baskets-full when done. You spin and twist the thread
just like Arachne (turned into a spider) or Penelope
(deserted); yet it's work some sweat-shop slag could do.

We all know why the late H. left his property

148

all to his freedman (also why he used to give his wife
so many gifts). Lady, just play three-in-a-bed
and you'll get rich. Wed him, keep quiet and take the
jewels.
Can you say anything against us women after that?
You blame the dove, but let the vulture off the hook!'

The pseudo-Stoics fled defeated when Miss X
was saying this, because she only spoke the truth.

But men *are* terrible. When you, my learned Mr C.,
appear in flimsy gear, they all applaud! Meanwhile
you thunder publicly against Miss So-and-So as an
adultress. Well, so are other women, but *they* would
never dress like that!
'July is hot!'
So do it naked! Barmy, but less shame attached.
Are those clothes suitable for handing down the law
to our victorious soldiers, fresh from battle, or
to mountain countrymen who've left the plough for you?
You'd soon complain if you should see a judge dressed up
like that. And would such flimsy garb suit witnesses?
You, Mr C., the sharp and learned champion
of liberty, wear see-through gear! It's sick, and it
will spread. You see it in the fields, when one sick sheep
or pig will cross-infect and kill the whole damn flock,
or mould will spread from grape to grape or bunch to
bunch.

Those clothes will lead you on to more outrageous things
(although it takes a time developing). You'll start
to visit houses where the clothes are very odd,
all necklaces and bows, cross-dressers sacrificing
to the Mother Goddess, mixing wine with pig's guts
in a great bowl. But in perverted ritual
it's now the women who may not come in, and men
alone approach her altar. 'Go away!' they shout,
'Unclean!' We want no high-pitched women fluting here!

They had such secret torchlight romps in Athens once,
to (over-)celebrate some Sex-Goddess from Thrace.
One man will use an eyebrow pencil, looking up
with lashes fluttering, to put his make-up on;
another drinks out of a glass shaped like a prick,
his tresses tied back in a golden net, and dressed
in clothes of pastel blue or palest green, and slaves
and masters both will swear 'By Juno,' not 'by Jove!'
Another man will have a mirror like the one
Otho, our narcissistic emperor used (a spoil
of war?) to check his armour before his last fight.
Now *there's* a thing to put down in the annals of
our times – a make-up mirror in a civil war!
A general really had to be on top to kill
his rival *and* keep his complexion fresh, to live
in palace luxury whilst on the battle-field,
and give himself a mud-pack for his face. The Queen
of Babylon, the archer-queen, never behaved
like that, and nor did Cleopatra at the end.
You won't find decent language or good manners there,
just dirty talk in pseudo-feminine falsetto,
while an ancient white-haired loony plays chief priest
(though's he's renowned as a master of gluttony –
he should give lessons!) One can only wonder why
they don't go all the way and chop their male bits off!

One famous name went through the marriage rites, and
gave a massive sum of cash to some musician chap
as dowry. They were blessed, and then they all sat down
to feast. The blushing 'bride' lay in her 'husband's' lap.

Now, do we need a censor, or someone to read
the omens? And how ominous and ghastly would you
think it, if a woman bore a calf, a cow a lamb?
That man, now dressed up in the bridal gown and veil,
once carried, sweating, in procession as a priest

of Mars, our sacred shields. O Father Romulus,
what made your shepherd-people so corrupt? O Mars!
where did your children get this stinging-nettle itch?
Just look! A man of birth and wealth is 'married' to
another *man*, and you don't twitch or shake your lance,
and don't complain to Father Jove! Scram! Leave the Field
of Mars (so-called), which you've forgotten!

'At first light tomorrow I must go to the Quirinal Valley.'
'What's on?' 'Why ask? Some chaps I know are getting
married. Just a small affair.' It won't be long
before these things get write-ups in the public press!
Meanwhile, however, there's one problem for these
brides – they can't have children (and so tie their husbands
down).
They want them badly. Thanks to Mother Nature, though,
their bodies can't comply. They'll die without issue,
in spite of foreign magic potions (they're no use!)
and taking part in rituals of fertility.

Worse still was when our so-called bride of noble birth
played net-man in a gladiatorial show in the
arena – a man whose lineage is superior
to most of the best families, and certainly
nobler than the spectators at the so-called games,
especially the one who paid to put them on.

Not even little boys (unless they're under five)
believe in ghosts, and Hades underneath the earth,
and frog-filled pools in Stygian darkness, and the Styx,
where thousands cross each day in one small boat.
But if they *do* exist, what would our honoured dead,
the shades of generals and consuls, think (or all
the men who fell in glorious battle, all those
military souls), if one of *this* lot should arrive

151

down there? They'd call for exorcism, if you could
drum up a bell, a candle and a book to do the job!

Alas, to what depths have we sunk! In arms we've
marched to Ireland, taken Orkney and dark Britain too,
but what the people do back in victorious Rome,
those conquered folk would never dream of! But a young
Armenian (we are told) is more effeminate
than our lot, and a Tribune is seducing *him*.
That's what bad influence can do. He came here as
a hostage; Rome made him grow up. A longer stay,
and boys like him will never lack a fancy-man.
They'll scrap their breeches, whips and knives and bridles,
and take back our noble Roman *mores* to their distant homes.

Cassius Dio

Commodus

Emperor AD 177–192

'If a man were to fix the period in the history of the world during which the condition of the human race was most happy and prosperous, he would, without hesitation, name that which elapsed from the death of Domitian to the accession of Commodus.'

So wrote Edward Gibbon in *The Decline and Fall of the Roman Empire*. And certainly, under the emperors Nerva, Trajan, Hadrian and the Antonines – the so called 'Adoptive Emperors' – the practice of an emperor adopting as his successor the man who seemed best qualified for the task led to a period of much more stable and enlightened rule. It was broken finally when the philosopher emperor, Marcus Aurelius, allowed his natural son, the hedonistic and megalomaniac Commodus, to succeed him. It was a difficult choice for Marcus. There were no obvious candidates for adoption without the risk of causing factional strife, and whoever might finally have succeeded him, it was unlikely that Commodus would have been allowed to survive. But with the accession of Commodus – who had the same devotion to playing the charioteer and gladiator as Nero had for playing the actor and singer – the Golden Age which Gibbon described came to an abrupt end.

CASSIUS DIO

From *The Roman History*

LXXIII, 17–21

Commodus would never drive a chariot in public except occasionally on nights when there was no moon, because although he really wanted to be a charioteer in public as well, he was ashamed to be seen at it. In private, however, he would often do it, wearing the livery of the Green racing-team. He killed a large number of wild beasts in private, and a large number in public as well. In addition, he would fight as a gladiator, and when he did so in private, he sometimes killed a man (and in battle with others, as if trimming their hair with a razor, he cut off their noses, or the ears or other parts). In front of the people, however, he would not use iron, nor spill men's blood. Before he went into the amphitheatre he wore a silk tunic of white and gold, with sleeves, and in that costume he received our greetings, but when he was due to go in, he put on a purple robe with gold embroidery, a Greek-style cloak of the same colour, and a golden crown with gemstones from India, and he carried a herald's staff, like Mercury. The lion-skin and club of Hercules were carried in front of him in the street, and in the theatre they were put on a gilded chair when he was present and also when he was not. He went into the arena dressed up as Mercury, and, having thrown off all his other garments, he set to work barefoot and wearing only the tunic.

On the first day he killed a hundred bears himself, throwing javelins down at them from the balustrade above; the theatre had been divided with two cross-walls, supporting the gallery that went all round it. The wild beasts were thus divided into four herds and could be speared easily from any point. What's more, in the middle of all this action Commodus became tired, and took a club-shaped cup of cold, sweet wine from a woman, and drank it all at one go. All the people, and we, the senators, at once shouted out the drinking-session formula: 'Health and Long Life to You!'

Now I do not want anyone to think I am dishonouring the dignity of history if I write down things like this. Normally, to be sure, I would not have mentioned this business, but it *was* done by the emperor himself, and I was there myself, witness to everything seen, heard or spoken, and so I have decided to suppress not a single thing, but to pass it all on, however trivial, for posterity. Furthermore, I shall describe all the events that happened during my lifetime more exactly and in more detail than earlier ones, because I was there when they happened, and I do not know of any other chronicler who is familiar with the events to the same extent as I am.

So that is what happened on the first day. On the others, he went down into the arena from his place up above and killed the animals that came near him, or were led in, or brought in nets; he killed a tiger, a hippopotamus and an elephant. After all this he would retire, but then after eating he would fight as a gladiator. The kind of fighting (and the equipment he had) was that of the so-called *secutor*, the swordsman. he had the shield in his right hand and a sword made of wood in his left — he was proud of being left-handed. Fighting against him was an athlete or gladiator, using a stave, either someone he had challenged himself, or someone chosen by the people. Here as in all other things he let himself be treated the same way as all the other gladiators, except that they fought for a few coins, and Commodus enriched himself with a colossal amount from the gladiatorial fund every day. Aemilius Laetus, the Praetorian Prefect, and also Eclectus, his chamberlain, were beside him when he was fighting, and when he had finished his bout (and won, of course), he used to kiss these, with his helmet on. And then the other gladiators would fight. The first day he himself arranged all the fights, down in the arena, dressed up as Mercury and carrying a gilded staff, and then he went onto a platform which was also gilded. This was regarded as an omen. And then he went to his usual place to watch the rest of the games with us. From now on the battles were no longer like children playing, but were serious, with a great many men killed. And once, when the winners were slow to kill those they had defeated, he tied the gladiators together and made them fight. The men fought against each other that way, and some killed men from different groups, because the numbers and the lack of space brought them so close together.

This kind of activity went on for a fortnight. When Commodus himself was in action, we senators and the Order of Knights were always present, and only Claudius Pompeianus the Elder never came, but stayed away and only sent his sons. He himself would rather be killed than watch the emperor, the child of Marcus Aurelius, behave in this manner. For among other things that we did, we had to shout slogans out on demand, especially (and frequently) 'You're the Lord! First and most blessed of all men! Victory is yours, and always shall be! Amazon, victory is yours!' But many of the ordinary people did not go into the amphitheatre, or they just looked in and then left, either from shame at what was happening, or from fear, because the word was that he wanted to fire arrows at some of the spectators, in imitation of Hercules when he killed the Stymphalian birds – and the story was believed, because he once gathered together all the men in the city who had lost their feet (by disease or accident), fixed serpent-like tails below their knees, gave them sponges to throw instead of stones, and then clubbed them to death, saying that they were monsters.

We shared this fear, just as much as the rest of the people. And he did another thing to us senators that made us fear our own deaths.

He killed an ostrich and cut off its head, and came to where we were sitting, holding the head in his left hand

and a bloody sword in the right; he said nothing, but shook his own head and smiled, indicating that he would treat us the same way. And many might have been cut down there and then for laughing at him — for it was laughter, not distress, that this provoked — if I had not started chewing on some leaves which I grabbed from my laurel-crown (and I got others nearby to do the same); the movement of our jaws hid the fact that we were really laughing.

Cassius Dio

The Accession of Didius Julianus

AD 193

Commodus was finally assassinated by members of his household. He was succeeded by Pertinax, who had been city prefect and whose energetic efforts to implement emergency financial and disciplinary reforms after the negligence of Commodus were resented by the Praetorian Guard. Founded by Augustus, the Praetorians were an elite body of guards upon whose might the power and authority of an emperor rested. But at this period they had become like a Frankenstein monster, a thing beyond their master's control. A fledgling emperor could not hold power in Rome without their support, and the Praetorians had begun to regard the throne itself as something within their gift. After a rule of only three months the soldiers murdered the unpopular Pertinax. This, and what followed, became one of the most lamentable episodes in Roman history.

LXXIV, 10–12 (The Accession of Didius Julianus)

The soldiers cut off the head of Pertinax, put it on a spear, and were cheered for doing so. And that is how Pertinax perished – a man who wanted to renew everything at once. In spite of his wide experience, he did not understand that it is not pragmatically possible to restore everything at a stroke, and that the renewal of an entire political system needs time and wisdom. He was four months and three days short of sixty-seven, and had reigned for eighty-seven days.

When it became known what had happened to Pertinax, some people hurried to their own homes, others to those of the soldiers, everyone having their own safety in mind. Flavius Sulpicianus, however, who had been sent to the Praetorian Camp by Pertinax to restore order, stayed where he was and tried to get himself acclaimed emperor. But when Didius Julianus (a wheeler-dealer and a wastrel, who was always ready to stir up political trouble and who had been exiled to his home city of Milan by Commodus), heard of the death of Pertinax, he went to the Camp, stood at the gates and tried to persuade the soldiers that *he* ought to rule over the Romans. What happened next was a very nasty piece of business indeed, and quite unworthy of Rome. For just as if it were a market-place or an sale-room, the city and the state were put up for auction, and those selling were the ones who had killed the emperor. The buyers were Sulpicianus and Julianus, outbidding each other, one from inside and one from outside. The bids rose as high as five thousand silver pieces per man; some of the guards would take word to Julianus and say 'Sulpicianus offers so much – what can you do instead?' Sulpicianus, who was already in the Camp, was a senior city official, and was the first to name that sum of five thousand silver pieces, would have won if Julianus had not upped his offers not just by a little, but by a very large amount at a time, which he shouted out in a great voice and also indicated with his hands. The soldiers, caught by his generous offer and also afraid (following a suggestion made by Julianus) that Sulpicianus might want to avenge Pertinax, brought Julianus in and declared him emperor.

And so, towards evening, the new ruler went to the Forum and to the Senate House, accompanied by a large number of the Guard, who were carrying their standards and seemed ready for action. He wanted to intimidate us, the senators and the people, and win us over that way. The soldiers were cheering him and calling him 'Commodus'. When word came to each of us senators, we were frightened of Julianus and the Guard, especially those of us that had done anything for Pertinax (and I was one of those myself – I had been honoured by Pertinax and made praetor, and when acting at trials for other people I had often found him – Julianus – to be guilty of offences). For all that, we did turn out, partly because staying at home did not seem safe and might have aroused suspicion. So after a bath and dinner we pushed our way through the soldiers, went into the House and heard his (predictable) speech, in which he said: 'I see that you need a ruler, and I myself am clearly best suited of anyone to take command. I would list all my good points if you did not already know them and if you hadn't already had experience of me. Therefore I did not ask to be accompanied by many soldiers, but have come here alone, so that you can confirm what they have given me.' He did say 'I am here alone,' although he had placed heavily armed Praetorians around the Senate and had many soldiers in the House itself. He also reminded us of the sort of man he was – and because of this we hated and feared him.

Apuleius

Born c. AD 120

Novelist

'The Golden Ass' of Apuleius is a delightful work, a novel of magic, adventure, bawdy humour, mythology and religion. It follows the misfortunes of one Lucius who, by means of sorcery, is transformed into an ass. The only antidote for this unhappy condition is to eat roses, but naturally this proves continually to be unfeasibly difficult. In this extract Lucius the Ass falls into the hands of a group of itinerant eunuchs, servants of the Syrian goddess Atargatis.

APULEIUS

from *Metamorphoses*, better known as *The Golden Ass*

VII, 15-IX, 10

Sighing deeply and weeping from time to time, he told his tale, and it affected the country people profoundly. Afraid of getting a new master, and very sorry about the misfortunes that had come upon their former master's house, they made plans to run away. The bailiff of horses, who had been so firmly charged with looking after me, took everything of value that he had in his little house, loaded it onto my back and onto the backs of the other pack animals, and left his former home. We were carrying children and women, chickens, sparrows, young goats and puppies; anything which would delay our escape by its weakness, used our legs instead of their own. But I was not worried about the weight of my burden, however massive, because it was welcome escape from that detestable person who wanted to chop off my manhood.

We crossed the scrubby ridge of a wooded mountain, and then the length of the plain beyond it, until at evening, just when it was getting dark, we reached a well-populated and prosperous little town, the residents of which would not let us go on that night, nor indeed leave in the morning. Apparently the whole region was overrun with bands of huge, strong wolves, who would attack with ferocious savagery; they would even lie in wait like highwaymen by the side of the road and set upon travellers. Starved and rabid, they would even attack farm-buildings, and the destruction of the defenceless farm-animals was now threatening humans as well. Then they told us that the whole route that we were going to take was strewn with half-devoured corpses, and that everywhere there were gleaming white bones stripped of their very flesh. They suggested that we should take up our travels again only with extreme care, and first of all to make sure that we did so in broad daylight, after dawn and in full sunshine, avoiding secret ambushes from both sides of the road (since the force of these dreadful beasts was reduced by sunlight), and proceeding not in Indian-file, but in wedge-formation; if we did that, we might surmount the difficulties.

But the useless leaders of our exodus, in blind and reckless haste, and fear of possible pursuit, disregarded this sound advice, and did not wait until the dawn of the following day, but loaded us up and ushered us out onto the road at around midnight. I myself was in terror of the dangers of which we had been warned, and hid amongst the thick crowd of pack animals to protect my backside as far as I could from the savagery of those wild wolves. Everyone marvelled at how swiftly I outran the rest of the horses; but this turn of speed had nothing to do with enthusiasm on my part, but was a sign of sheer terror. Then it occurred to me that even the famous Pegasus must have been driven to flight primarily by fear, and had earned the description 'winged' when he jumped up and rose into the sky because he was terrified of a bite from the fire-breathing Chimaera. Even the herdsmen driving us had armed themselves, as if for a battle, one with a spear, one with a javelin, another with a throwing-dart, another a club, and some even with the stones which the roadway so generously provided for us. Some carried sharpened stakes, and most of them were carrying burning torches to frighten off the wild beasts. The only thing we did not have was a trumpet, or we'd have been just like an army on the march.

But our fears proved unfounded, and we did it all in vain, although the trap we fell into was far worse. None of the wolves came near us, and we never even saw one in the distance; possibly they were confused by the racket of all these young men, or frightened off by the light of the flames, or perhaps they were just off somewhere else.

166

However, the people on a farmstead that we happened to be passing thought from our numbers that we must be brigands, and so, afraid for their property, they set their huge and vicious dogs on us, dogs that were more savage than wolves or bears, and which they had trained to protect them, urging them onto us with shouts and all kinds of noise. The innate savagery of these dogs was aggravated by the noise their owners were making, so they rushed at us, surrounded us and jumped on us from all sides, tearing at pack-animals and at men indiscriminately for so long that they had brought down nearly all of us. What a sight – though the whole show was more pitiful than memorable! All those slavering, excited hounds, some chasing those who had tried to run away, others holding onto those who had stood still, and lots prowling around our whole group, snapping and snarling!

And after this horror there was much worse to follow. The farmers began to throw rocks down onto us from their roofs and from a nearby hilltop, so that we didn't know which we needed to take cover from the most, the dogs on top of us, or the rocks aimed at us. One of the latter struck the head of the woman who was sitting on my back. At once she started to weep and scream in pain, and called out for her husband, the bailiff, to help her. He called on heaven to protect him, wiped the blood from his wife's head and called out, 'Why are you attacking and hurting us weary and wretched travellers so viciously? What do you expect to get out of it? What kind of revenge are you taking? Are you wild beasts living in hollows, or cave-dwelling barbarians, that you take pleasure in spilling human blood?

Hardly had he said this, when the shower of rocks stopped at once, the savage dogs were called off and the storm subsided. One of the men then shouted down from the top of a cypress tree, 'no, we are not thieves who want to rob you; we were only trying to stop you doing the same thing to us. You can go on now, in peace and quiet.'

And that was that. But we took up our journey with a

lot of wounds, some from rocks, some from the jaws of the hounds, but everyone was hurt somehow. When we had gone along the road a little way, we came to a grove with tall trees and pleasant grassy meadows, and our leaders said that we should rest for a little while to recover and look after the various wounds that our bodies had received. And so first of all everyone lay around to recover, and then they all made efforts to heal their wounds in different ways, some washing off the blood in the stream that ran through the place, others putting vinegar-soaked sponges on their bruises, still others bandaging their cuts. In this fashion, everyone looked after themselves.

While this was going on, an old man saw us from the top of a hill, and the fact that had nanny-goats feeding all round him indicated rather clearly that he was a herdsman. One of our people asked him if he had any fresh milk or buttermilk to sell. He shook his head for a long time, and said, 'can you really be thinking of eating or drinking, or any other refreshments just now? Surely you must know where it is that you are camping?' And having said that, he rounded up his flocks, turned round, and went. His words, and his precipitous exit aroused not a little terror in our people. Scared as they were, they tried to find out what kind of place this was, but there was no-one to tell them, until another old man came long the road, a large man, weighed down with years, bent right down over his stick, shuffling along and weeping as he did so. When he saw us, he prostrated himself, weeping copiously, before our young men and addressed them imploringly.

'By all the lucky fates and guardian angels that watch over you, may you reach my age healthy and happy, and help a poor old man snatch his little one from the jaws of hell and give him back to me, grey-haired as I am. You see, my grandson, my sweet travelling companion, was trying to catch a sparrow that happened to be singing in the hedge when he fell into a nearby pit behind the bushes. His life is now in extreme danger, and I know he is still alive by his weeping and his voice, calling over and over again for his grandfather. As you see, I cannot help him because I am old and weak. But, with the benefit of your youth and strength, you would find it easy to help a poor old man, and save the youngest boy of my line, indeed, my only heir, for me.'

Everyone was sorry for him as he told us all this, tearing at his grey hair. But then one of our men, braver, younger and stronger than the others, and the only one who had escaped unharmed from the earlier battle, leapt up and asked where the boy had fallen. He then set off energetically with the old man, who was pointing at some spiky bushes a little way away. When the people had seen to their wounds, and had fed us beasts, everyone picked up their packs to set off on our way. First of all they shouted out the young man's name several times, and then soon afterward – worried about the delay – they sent one of their men to look for the one who was missing, to tell him it was time to move on, and bring him back. But this man soon returned, ashen-faced and shaking, and reported a strange tale about his fellow. He had seen him lying down on his back, with a great snake on top of him which had almost eaten him up; there was no sign of that most unhappy old man. When this sank in, and was taken together with the words of the old goatherd (who had presumably been warning us against none other than the monstrous dweller in that grove), they fled even faster from that terrible region, hitting us hard with their sticks. Then, when we had done a long day's journey as fast as we could, we reached a village where we stayed a whole night. I should like to give an account of a most notable ghastly deed that had happened in that town.

There was a slave whose master had put the stewardship of the whole household into his hands, and who therefore had had control of the whole estate where we were staying; he was married to another slave owned by the same family, but was consumed with passion for a freedwoman who came from somewhere else. The wife, tormented and spurred on by her husband's faithlessness, burned all his records and everything he had kept in the storehouse. Nor was this damage enough to avenge the shame brought upon her marriage; she now turned against the fruit of her own womb, and tied a noose round her neck, and tied to the same rope the tiny baby that she had just borne her husband, and hurled herself into a deep well, dragging the baby with her on the rope. The master was very upset about these deaths, seized the slave whose licentious behaviour had been the cause of such a ghastly happening, and tied him firmly, naked and smeared all over with honey, to a fig-tree, in the rotten trunk of which were many seething ants'-nests, whose inhabitants bubbled out like a stream. As soon as the ants noticed the sweet smell of honey on his body, they attacked his skin with tiny but constant bites, and after a long time of torture, the man died. His flesh, and even his intestines were eaten away, so that only his bare bones, stripped of flesh and shining white, were still tied to that tree of doom.

We got out of this horrible stopping-place too, leaving the local people in the depths of sorrow, and walked across the flatlands all day until we reached, exhausted, a city that was fine and well-populated. Here our herdsmen decided to set up home, because it seemed like a safe refuge from anyone who might be sent out to look for them – it was a long way away – and because the plentiful supply of food was also attractive. And so, after three days rest, to get the bodies of the pack-animals back into shape, and make us look more saleable, we were taken to the market, where the auctioneer shouted out the price of each beast in a loud voice and where the horses and other asses were sold to rich buyers. But I was left over, and most people just passed over me with disdain. By now I was fed up with people trying to guess how old I was from my teeth, and when a man whose hand was filthy and smelly anyway kept running his grubby fingers over my gums I caught his hand and nearly bit it off. This acted as a deterrent to any buyer, since I was clearly particularly ferocious, so that the salesman, now suffering from a sore throat and with his voice going, started to make silly jokes about me. 'How long do we keep this old gelding up here waiting? The poor old bugger's hooves are worn out, he's all twisted, and his idleness is positively vicious! He's not much more than a garbage-can. So why don't we just give him away to someone or other who doesn't mind wasting hay!'

The auctioneer got a laugh from the bystanders with remarks like this. However, my personal and sadistic Lady Luck – whom I had not so far been able to escape by fleeing through so many lands, and whom I had not been able to placate with my sufferings so far – once again failed to notice, let alone smile at me, and provided for me a purchaser who was just about what I needed for the dire state I was in. What about this, then: a sodomite, nay, an *old* sodomite, more or less bald, but with a few locks of hair still dangling on his head, a specimen of those vulgar and common types who wander around cities and country towns with cymbals and rattles, carrying the Syrian goddess Atargatis and degrading her by begging in her name. He was keen to buy me, and asked the auctioneer where I might be from; he told him that I was one of those strong fellows from Cappadocia, and swore I was a tough little chap. The next question was my age.

To this the auctioneer replied, with a twinkle in his eye, 'an astrologer who cast his horoscope reckons he is in his fifth year, but he probably knows better himself from filling in his tax forms. However, even though I'm well aware that I shall be guilty of an offence under the act if I sell you a Roman citizen as a slave, why not buy this fine and useful fellow anyway, who will be of the greatest help to you at home and on the road?'

But the odious would-be-purchaser would not stop putting questions, and eventually asked anxiously about my general temperament.

'What you see before you,' said the salesman, 'is a wether, a sheep, not an ass; doesn't bite, doesn't kick, and you could easily believe that inside this ass's skin there lived a good-mannered, well-brought-up man. It shouldn't

171

be difficult to convince yourself, however. Why don't you just stick you face up between his back legs – you'll soon find out the extent of his patience.'

The auctioneer had his laugh at the expense of the fat fool, but he joined in with the joke and pretended to be angry. 'You complete dead-head,' he said, 'you donkey-selling pillock! May the all-powerful, Syrian goddess, mother of all, the holy god Sabazius, and Bellona, and the Mother-Goddess of Mount Ida and Attis her eunuch companion, and Venus and Adonis too, may they all strike you blind for wasting my time with your stupid jokes! You asshole, do you think that I could let the goddess be carried by some wild beast who might tip the holy image off his back, so that I, poor little sweetie that I am, would have to run around with my hair all over the place and look for a doctor for my fallen goddess?'

Hearing that, I did wonder about leaping up suddenly like a mad thing, so that he wouldn't buy me when he saw how wild I was. But the over-eager buyer pre-empted this idea by putting down his cash on the table, which the auctioneer took at once, since he was fed up with me: seventeen denarii. He put a rope-bridle on me and gave me to Philebus, this being the name of my new master.

Philebus took possession of his newly acquired helper and dragged me off home. As soon as we reached the door he shouted out, 'Girls, here's a pretty little slave boy I've brought home for you.' But the 'girls' were really a mob of perverts, who at once danced about with delight and shouted in their cracked, nasty and effeminate voices, presumably thinking that I really was some human slave-lad brought home for their use. But when they saw me, not a doe like the one they substituted for Iphigenia when she was going to be sacrificed, but an ass as a substitute for a man, they turned up their noses and started to cavil at their leader, saying that this was a husband he'd brought home for himself, not a slave. 'Come on,' they said, 'mind you don't gobble up your pretty little chickadee all by yourself – make sure you give your little lovie-dovies a bit every now and then!'

In the middle of all this joking, they took me and tied me near the manger. They also owned a rather solid young man (who was a good musician) that they had bought with money they had collected, and who walked ahead when they were carrying the goddess about, playing a horn. At home, however, he played the part of communal bedfellow. As soon as he saw me in the house he was delighted, and gave me a huge helping of fodder. 'At last,' he said, 'someone to help me out in my terrible work. Make sure you live for a long time and please our owners, and give my weary loins a chance!' When I heard this, I began to wonder about what new problems I was going to have.

The following day they put on brightly coloured clothes and prettied themselves up horribly by putting caked make-up on their faces and exaggerating their eyes with eye-shadow, and set out, wearing pointed hats and saffron robes in linen or silk; some had white tunics with a design of purple lines all over them and with a tight belt, and they had yellow sandals on their feet. The goddess, wrapped in a silk cover, was put on my back so I could carry her, and they, with arms completely bare, and worked up by the playing of the music, whirled and chanted, waving monstrous swords and axes.

After going past a few small places, they reached the farmstead of a well-off land-owner, and as soon as they reached the entrance-hall they hurtled forward frantically, with their discordant yelling, and then for a long time they put their heads down and swung their necks round and round in circles, with their hair flying out around their heads. Some of them bit into their own flesh, and eventually they all started slashing their arms with the blades they were carrying. One of them got into more of a wild state than the others, breathing great gasps from deep down in his chest as if filled with some kind of divine inspiration, and generally simulating a crazed ecstasy. Of course, the immanence of the gods is supposed to make men improve, not make them weaker or demented. However, now just

173

look at the reward he got from divine providence. Shouting out like a soothsayer he began in lying fashion to accuse and incriminate himself, saying he had somehow broken some very holy religious law, and he demanded proper punishment for his crime from his own hands. He grabbed hold of one of the scourges that is a trademark of this barely human cult – long, and made of strips of plaited sheepskin with pieces of bone knotted into it – and rained blows from the knotted parts onto himself, bearing the pain with amazing fortitude. You could see the ground becoming wet from this pansy's blood, as it spurted out from all the lashing and slashing. I was not a little afraid to see all these wounds and all that blood, and wondered whether this well-travelled Syrian goddess might have a taste for ass's blood, the way men sometimes have a fancy for ass's milk.

But when at last they were tired, or had had enough of flagellation, they stopped this mortification of the flesh and took a collection of small change, although many people gave them silver as well (which they collected in their robes), to say nothing of the jar of wine, the milk, the cheeses, grain and wheat-flour – some even gave barley for the beast carrying the goddess. They took it all greedily and stuffed it into the bags they had ready, and put it onto my back, so that now I had double the weight to carry; I was a storehouse *and* a temple at the same time.

In this manner they wandered around and milked the entire district. One day, however, when they were in a largish town and had had a bigger take than usual, they set a great banquet up for themselves. Using a concocted bit of soothsaying they conned out of one of the farmers his fattest ram, supposedly a sacrifice for the hungry Syrian goddess, and when they had arranged for their dinner, they went to the baths and came back bringing with them a guest, a hefty country chap, strong in limbs and loins. Having eaten only a little salad as a starter before the main meal, these most disgusting creatures were soon burning with wild desire for crimes of illicit lust, and surrounded the young man (who had been stripped and spread-eagled), with their filthy mouths all over him. My eyes could not watch such horrors for long, so I tried to shout out 'Help! Horrors!' but only managed 'He . . . Horr' and lost all the other syllables, but at least it was loud, clear and ass-like, although somewhat inopportune as to timing. For a group of young men from a nearby village were looking for an ass stolen that very night, and were looking into all the taverns, so that when they heard me braying in there they though that their stolen ass was hidden indoors. Wanting to get their property back they broke in on us, and caught the disgusting crew at it, performing their vile acts. They very quickly indeed roused the whole neighbourhood to come and see the abominable scene, mocking the priests for their pure chastity.

Greatly concerned by the scandal (of which word soon got around, and which made them look deservedly revolting to everyone), they got their things together and left the town furtively around midnight. A good part of their journey was done before daybreak, and by the time it was fully light they were in a remote district, where they held a discussion and then girded their loins – and that was my funeral! They took the goddess off my back and put her on the ground, stripped me of all my gear, tied me to an oak-tree and flogged me with their plaited whip (the one with the bones in it) until I was practically dead. One of them threatened to hamstring me with an axe because I had shouted out so vigorously about his supposedly snow-white virtue. But the rest decided that I should be kept alive, not for my own sake, but for that of the statue, which was currently lying on the ground. And so I was loaded up again and bullied with the flats of their swords until they got to a fine town. One of the town councillors there, a religious man with a special veneration for the Syrian goddess, was excited by the ring of the cymbals, the sounds of the drums and the exotic song with its captivating melodies, and ran out to meet us. He received the goddess with pious generosity, and gave us rooms in his extremely large house, trying to win divine favour with the greatest reverence and the best sacrifices.

I remember that it was here that I ran into especially great danger. One of the tenant farmers had been hunting, and had sent as a present for his master a fine and massive haunch of venison, which had been hung rather stupidly by the kitchen door not very high up, so that another hunter – a dog, this time – had rushed in and stolen it; delighted with his booty, he had made sure he got out of everyone's sight. The cook cursed his own carelessness when he saw the loss, and wept useless tears, but his master was already calling urgently for his dinner. The despairing and terrified cook said farewell to his small son and got a noose ready for his own neck. However, his faithful wife – aware of the seriousness of her husband's situation – grabbed the fatal rope with both hands and said, 'Have you been scared completely out of your wits by this trouble? Surely you can see the lucky remedy that divine providence had found for you? If you want to see the silver lining in the dark cloud of fate, snap out of it and listen to me! Get that ass which has just turned up, take it round the corner somewhere, slit its throat and cut a haunch to look like the one that went missing. If you cook it well in a special spicy sauce, you can still serve it to the master in place of the venison.

The idea of saving his skin with my life appealed to the wretched man, and with much praise for the bright idea of his wife, he started to sharpen the knives ready for this butchery.

So there was this dreadful executioner arming his ungodly self against me! But spurred on by the extreme danger I was in, I didn't hang about thinking, but decided to escape from the imminent carve-up by running away. So I swiftly snapped the rope that was holding me and bolted at top speed to save myself, my hooves flying. I got across the forecourt, and burst precipitously (and not without knocking over quite a few tables, braziers and other bits of dining-room furniture) into the room where the master of the house was entertaining the priests of the goddess to a sacrificial feast. The head of the house was most put out at the mess, and called me an uncontrollable and wicked beast; he then told a servant to lock me up somewhere so that I didn't disturb their quiet dinner again with a repetition of this outburst. Saved from the butcher's hands by this jolly cunning little trick, I was very happy about this prison which would save me.

However, nothing can turn out right for any man alive if fate is against him, and neither good advice nor clever plans can possible change or modify divine providence. For me, you see, that which seemed to have given me instant salvation led to another great danger, which put me in peril of my life.

A lad suddenly burst suddenly into the dining-room, his face trembling and twitching, while the guests were chatting quietly, and told his master that a rabid bitch had just run in amazingly fast through the back gate from a nearby lane, and burning with wild rage had attacked the hunting-dogs, then gone on to the stables and attacked most of the pack-animals just as savagely. Not even the humans had been spared; Myrtilus the muleteer, Hephaestio the cook, Hypnophilus the chamberlain and Apollonius the doctor had all been bitten in more than one place, as had many others, while trying to get rid of the bitch. Many of the pack-animals that had been bitten and infected were apparently already showing signs of rabies. This news left everybody stunned, and they assumed that I, too, had been affected by the disease, so they grabbed whatever implements they could and came after me, encouraging each other to get rid of this common death-sentence, although *they* were the ones suffering from the disease of lunacy. Nor do I have any doubt that they would have cut me into little pieces with their lances, spears and double-headed axes (which the servants quickly provided for them), had I not seen this storm of danger coming and rushed rapidly into the bedroom of my masters. Then they locked and barred the doors on me, and besieged the place, to wait for me to develop and be consumed with this lethal rabies, without any danger of infection to themselves. So once again I was free, and grasped this gift of fate very firmly: I lay down on one of their beds and for the first time in ages had a good human sleep.

I got up late – it was already daylight – with my tiredness soothed away by the softness of the bed, and listened to the men who had been keeping guard outside my room all night talking about my case. 'Is that wretched ass still tossing around in a crazed state, do we think?' Surely not! The sickness must have reached a crisis and have worn itself out by now. They decided to stop guessing and have a look, peered through a crack and saw me standing at my ease, quite calm and healthy. Then they opened the door to make more certain that I was, indeed, by now a gentle beast. One of them (clearly sent by the gods to help me!) said to the rest that one way of testing my sanity would be to give me a bowl of fresh water to drink, and if I drank it fearlessly and of my own accord, as usual, they would know that I was cured and well again. On the other hand, if I were to shudder and shy away from the sight of or contact with the water, then they would be sure that the terrible disease of rabies was still holding on. This was the normal text-book procedure for finding out.

It was reckoned to be a good idea, so they brought a vast bowl of beautifully clear water from a handy fountain and gave it to me, somewhat hesitantly. Without the slightest delay I went up to them, bobbed down (because I was really thirsty), shoved my entire head into the bowl and gulped that quite literally life-saving water. After that I let them pat me and play with my ears and pull on my rope and do any other test they liked, until – against their presumption that I was mad – I had made clear that I was perfectly tame.

In this way I had escaped two dangers, and the next day I was loaded up with all their religious clobber and led off on my way again with castanets and cymbals – the old travelling religious circus again. Having stopped at a good few isolated houses or small estates, we stopped in some village or other, built (so the inhabitants told us) in the dilapidated remains of what was once a fine, rich city, and got lodgings at the first tavern we came to. Here we got to hear a most entertaining tale about some poor chap and his wife's adultery, which I should like you to hear as well.

The man in question was really poor and struggling, and just kept his head above water with cheap-rate joinery jobs. His darling wife was as badly-off as he was financially, but was well-known for her rampant libido. One day, when he had gone out early to work on a job, his wife's rather bold lover came secretly into the house. While the pair were engaged in a spot of horizontal jogging, the husband – who neither knew nor even suspected that anything was up – came home unexpectedly. Finding the doors locked and barred, he praised his wife's virtue, knocked, and at the same time announced his presence by whistling. The woman was both clever and used to misbehaviour, so she disentangled herself from the man and hid him in a huge wine-vat in the corner of the room, half-covered in grime, but empty. When she unbarred the door and her husband came in, she really let him have it.

'What the hell do you think you're doing, idling about with your hands in your pockets and not thinking about how we are going to manage and not doing any work to make sure we can eat! And all the time I'm stuck here day and night wearing my fingers to the bone spinning wool just so we can keep the little lamp lit over the front door of our little house. That Daphne next door, now, she's a lot luckier than I am, spending her mornings drinking and nibbling and playing about with her lovers!'

Her husband was very put out. 'What do you mean?' he said, 'Our boss has had to appear in court, and has given us the day off, but I've still sorted out today's dinner for us. You see that great wine-vat? – it's always empty and it doesn't do anything except get in our way here. So I've sold it to somebody for five denarii, and he's coming round to pay me and pick up his purchase. While we are waiting why don't you give me a hand and help me get it ready to hand over to the man who's buying it?'

But the crafty woman was quite up to this one, gave a derisive laugh, and said, 'what a great husband, what a splendid salesman this one is! I'm only a woman, but even staying indoors I've already sold it for *seven* denarii, and he accepted less!'

Highly pleased at the increase in the price, the husband said, 'so who is it that's paid so much?'

'Idiot!' she replied, 'he's just climbed into the thing to check how solid it is.'

The lover didn't fail to follow the woman's lead. He quickly got out of the vat and said, 'tell you what, lady – see this vat of yours? It's pretty old, and there are cracks all over it.' And then, keeping up the pretence, he turned to the husband and said, 'come on, mate, whoever you are, nip off and get me a lamp so I can scrape off the dirt inside this to see if it's still usable! Money doesn't grow on trees, you know.'

But without hesitation or suspicion our quick-witted husband lit the lamp and said, 'just stand aside and take it easy, old chap, while I get it into shape for you to see.' And with that he stripped off, took the lamp into the vat and began to scrape away the filth from the old rotten inside walls.

Then the good-looking lover up-ended the work-man's wife over the curve of the vat and did indeed take it (and her) easily. Meanwhile, she stuck her head over the top of the vat and mocked her husband like a really crafty whore, indicating the parts that needed a good seeing-to – here, and here, and there, and then another one – until both jobs were well and truly done. Then the seven denarii changed hands, but the unfortunate workman still had to heave the vat onto his back and cart it across to the lover's house.

After our most pure priests had stayed there for a few days, and had got what they could in the way of public money and stuffed their pockets with the profit of prophecies, they thought of a new ploy. They worked out a single all-purpose prophecy, and that way they tricked all the people who came to ask about different things. It was this:

The oxen, yoked together, plough the furrows long,
to bring forth future fertile seedlings, young and strong.

That way, when someone questioned them when they were planning a marriage, say, they would assure them that this was a favourable utterance – the business about yoking was clearly conjugal, and the seedlings were the children that would come from it. If the questioner was wanting to buy property, then of course 'yoked oxen,' and 'long furrows' as well as fertile growth was prophesied. If someone was worried and wanted divine auguries before setting out on a journey, then the yoked oxen became the most dependable of beasts, while the bit about fertile seedlings promised a profitable outcome. If someone was going into battle or was setting off to chase bandits, and didn't know whether or not it would be worth it, then the good old prophecy presaged a victory: the necks of the enemy would come under the yoke, and the captives would yield rich and fertile booty.

In this way, with crafty soothsaying they got together no little amount of money. But they got fed up with all the questions and answers, and again set off on the road. This journey was far worse than any of the night-time ones, and why? because the road was rutted and the holes filled with stagnant water, and it was slippery with muddy slime in other places. My legs hurt from all that knocking into things and constant slipping, and I was tired out and hardly able to walk when we made it to a level road. But here we were suddenly overtaken by a group of armed horsemen, who reined in their mounts from their mad gallop and went viciously for Philebus and his companions, grabbing them by the throats, beating them, and calling them sacrilegious scum. Then they put manacles on the lot of them and kept on demanding that they should hand over at once the golden chalice, give up their principal piece of criminally-acquired loot, stolen from the shrine of the Mother Goddess when they were conducting a service behind closed doors; and then – as if they thought they could get away scot-free after such a crime – they had left town in the morning before it was properly light! One of the riders then put his hand over my back, felt around in the shrine of the goddess that I was carrying, and produced for everyone to see the golden chalice itself. Even in the face of such criminal sacrilege, these wretches were not afraid, but pretended to laugh it off, and said, "what rotten luck! It's always the innocent who get into situations like this! Because of one little cup, which the Mother Goddess gave her Syrian sister as a thanks-offering, ministers of religion are arrested and find themselves threatened just like common criminals." '

They went on babbling things like this, but all in vain, because the villagers took them back and put them in jail in chains. They returned the chalice and the goddess that I had been carrying to the temple with all reverence, and on the next day took me out and put me up for sale again, when I was bought for seven sesterces more than Philebus had paid, by a miller from the next town, who loaded me up with the grain he had also just bought, and led me off to his mill up a steep path with lots of sharp stones and tangled roots.

The Augustan History

Life of Heliogabalus

(ruled AD 218–222)

The Augustan History is a series of imperial biographies which cover the period AD 117–284. It was ostensibly written by six authors in the late 3rd and early 4th centuries and at intervals is addressed to the emperors Diocletian and Constantine. However, it is generally believed that this is a facade, and that it is truly the work of a single author probably written in the late 4th century. The book contains many fictions, but these are generally easier to disentangle than the fictions surrounding the work itself.

No study of Roman decadence could be complete without reference to the emperor Heliogabalus, surely the most bizarre of them all. His true name was Varius Avitus Bassianus Marcus Aurelius Antoninus, but history has known him as Elagabalus, or in the Greek, Heliogabalus, this being the name of the sun god in whose temple at Emesa (modern Homs) in Syria he served in the hereditary position of high priest. His grandmother Maesa was sister to the wife of the emperor Septimius Severus, who founded the Severan dynasty and finally dragged Rome from the mire into which it had sunk following the death of Commodus. When Severus died he was succeeded by his two sons, Caracalla and Geta. After a period of intense rivalry and animosity between the two brothers, Caracalla murdered Geta and ruled despotically until finally assassinated through a plot by Macrinus, his Praetorian commander, who then succeeded him as emperor.

Macrinus made a grave mistake, however, in allowing Caracalla's Syrian relatives to return to their ancestral temple at Emesa, where they were quick to take advantage of the soldiers' fond memories of Caracalla – who had always been generous to his troops at the expense of other sections of the Roman populace – and at their growing disaffection towards Macrinus. The fourteen year old Heliogabalus was presented by night in the camp of the 3rd legion, who were easily won over by his beauty and resemblance to Caracalla whose bastard he was claimed to be, as well as by the gifts and promises of his wealthy grandmother. Heliogabalus was quickly proclaimed emperor by the rebellious troops. Macrinus sent his soldiers against the insurgents, but only found that more of them were coerced into desertion. Eventually the rebel army engaged the loyal troops of Macrinus outside Antioch. During a desperate battle Macrinus' nerve seems to have failed, and he fled, soon to be hunted down and dispatched.

So began the scandalous four year reign of the exotic and epicene boy emperor named Heliogabalus after his god – the author of this biography, Lampridius, refers to both emperor and god by the same name. The image of the god, a black stone, was carried from his temple in Emesa to Rome, that his priest, the emperor, might promote his outlandish worship in the capital.

AELIUS LAMPRIDIUS

from the *Augustan History*

Antoninus Heliogabalus

I would have refrained from committing to paper the life of Antoninus Heliogabalus (also known as Varius), thus preventing anyone from finding out that he had ruled Rome, had it not been for the fact that the same imperial office had been held before him by the likes of Caligula, Nero and Vitellius. However, the earth brings forth poisons as well as grain and other useful things, and gives us serpents as well as domestic beasts. Bearing this in mind, the discerning reader can find a balance to these monstrous tyrants by reading about Augustus, Trajan, Vespasian, Hadrian, Antoninus Pius, Titus and Marcus Aurelius. That way, the reader will see that Rome really *is* capable of showing judgement, because all of the latter not only ruled for a long time, but also died of natural causes. The others, however, were killed and their bodies dragged through the streets, and were even known to be tyrants – nobody even cares now to mention their names.

After the emperor Macrinus and his son, Diadumenian (who shared with him the imperial throne, and who had taken the name Antoninus as well) had both been killed, Varius Heliogabalus was made emperor for the sole reason that he was supposed to be the son of Caracalla. However, he was really the priest of Elah-Gabal (or Jove, or the Sun-God), and he had simply assumed the Antonine name, either to establish a family connection, or because he knew that the name was so popular with the masses that because of it they even loved Caracalla, who had killed his own brother. Our man was originally called Varius, and was known later as Heliogabalus, from his priesthood of the god Elah-Gabal. He brought the god with him from Syria, and built a temple to him in Rome in a place which had originally had a shrine to the god of the Other-World. Once he assumed imperial power he was known as Antoninus, the last of the Antonine emperors.

He was so much under the control of his mother, Julia Soaemias, that he carried out no official business without her agreement, even though she had the *mores* of a street-walker and went in for all kinds of licentious behaviour while at court – her sexual relationship with Caracalla was so well-known that it was generally reckoned that this Varius, or Heliogabalus, actually *was* his son. But some people even went as far as to say that the name *Varius* was given to him by his classmates at school, because he seemed to have been conceived from the seed of *various* different men, which is what you would expect with a whore. After his putative father, Caracalla, had been killed in the Macrinus coup, he took refuge in the temple of the god Elah-Gabal, taking sanctuary there so that he would not be killed by Macrinus, who, together with his wanton and cruel son, was wielding power in a most savage fashion. But that's enough about what he was called, even though he defiled the much venerated name of the Antonines – a name which you, most revered Constantine, hold so dear that you have placed Marcus Aurelius and Antoninus Pius in gold amongst the Constantii and the Claudians, as if they had been your own ancestors, taking on the virtues of men of old which are appropriate to your own way of life, and which you find pleasing and worthy of love.

To come back to Varius Antoninus Heliogabalus: once he had gained the purple, he sent envoys to Rome, where all the different ranks and classes were enthusiastic – the whole populace, in fact, in whom a great longing for him was kindled simply by the Antonine name, not just as a title (as had been the case with Diadumenian), but because the family line seemed to be restored when he signed himself as the son of Antoninus Bassianus Caracalla. He enjoyed the prestige, too, which is given to a new ruler who comes after a tyrant has been removed, but this only lasts when the new ruler really *is* of the best character, and many a third-rate ruler has lost it.

Anyway, when the words sent by Heliogabalus were read out in the Senate, right away good wishes were offered 'for Antoninus,' while Macrinus and his son were cursed, and this Antoninus was declared emperor because everyone wanted him and believed in him. This is what happens with the prayers of people eager to believe something that they want to be the truth.

However, once he had entered the city he ignored everything that was going on in the rest of the empire, and established the religion of Elah-Gabal, building a temple for him on the Palatine, right next to the imperial palace, and wanting to move the emblem of the Mother Goddess, the Vestal fire, the image of Pallas, the sacred shields, and all the other things revered by the Romans, into that temple. He wanted to do this so that no other god but Elah-Gabal should be worshipped in Rome. He also said that the rites of the Jews, the Samaritans and the Christians should be transferred there too, so that the priesthood of Elah-Gabal could control the mysteries of all other cults.

Then, at the first meeting of the Senate, he commanded that his mother should be invited to attend. When she arrived she was given a seat with the consuls, and was present at a drafting, that is, she was a witness the formulation of a senatorial edict. This was the only emperor under whom a woman entered the Senate like a man, as if she were an actual senator.

He also established on the Quirinal a senatorial annexe or 'Senate for women.' In former times a congregation of married ladies had met there, albeit on special festivals, or whenever some married lady was being awarded the insignia of a 'consular marraige,' which is what emperors did in the old days for their female relatives, especially those whose husbands were not actually of the nobility, so that they did not therefore lose their rank. But Julia Soaemias saw to it that the Senate now enacted ridiculous decrees, passing laws concerning married women – how they could dress when they went out, who should give precedence to whom, who could come forward and kiss whom, who could ride in a carriage, on a palfrey, on a pack-horse, or on an ass, who could use a carriage drawn by oxen or by mules, who could be carried in a litter (and whether it could be made of leather or bone, or have ivory or gold decoration), and who would be allowed to have gold or jewels on her shoes.

After he had spent the winter in Nicomedia, therefore, indulging in all kinds of sordid behaviour, including sodomizing and being sodomized, the soldiers quickly came to regret having conspired against Macrinus and having made this man emperor, and they thought about Severus Alexander, a cousin of Heliogabalus whom the Senate had hailed as 'Caesar,' when Macrinus was killed. For who could possible stand an emperor who enjoyed lustful gratification through every orifice – even a beast which behaved like that would not be tolerated. When in Rome, too, he constantly sent out emissaries to look for men who were especially well-hung, and had them brought to the court so that he could enjoy what they had to offer. What's more, he used to act out the story of Paris in his house, he himself playing the role of Venus; then he would suddenly let his garments fall to his feet, and would kneel forward, naked, one hand on his breast and the other cupping his genitals, his bottom stuck up in the air and thrust back towards his bum-boy. He also used to make his face look like the way Venus is usually painted, and he had all his bodily hair removed, because he thought the highest enjoyment in life was to appear fit and ready for any number of libidinous delights.

He used to sell honours, distinctions and positions of power, either directly, doing so himself, or indirectly through his slaves or his fancy-men. He elevated people to the Senate regardless of age, land-ownership or family, just on the basis of cash payment, and not only were the ranks of captain, tribune, legate and general for sale, but even those of procurator, or of palace officials. The charioteers Protogenes and Carius, originally friends of his from the race-track, were later retained as his close associates in all areas of his life. He brought to court a good number of people from the theatre, the race-track or the ring because their bodies pleased him. Indeed, he was so besotted with a man called Hierocles that he used – it's hardly proper to mention it – to kiss his privates; he claimed that he was 'celebrating Carnival.'

He committed technical incest by violating a Vestal Virgin, and profaned what the Romans held most sacred when he shifted the holy shrines. He wanted to extinguish the sacred flame, and it was not only the Roman religious practices that he wanted to extinguish, but those of everybody else, his sole desire being to have the god Elah-Gabal worshipped everywhere. Moreover, unclean himself in every way possible, and accompanied by others who had defiled themselves, he forced a way into the inner sanctum of the Vestals, where only the virgins and their priests are permitted to go. He tried to take away the sacred vessel, but he stole only an earthenware copy, which the Chief Vestal had shown him as a trick, as if it were the real one, and when he found there was nothing in it he hurled it down and smashed it. However, he did not in fact deprive the Vestals of anything, because it is said that several identical vessels had been made, so that no-one could be sure of taking away the real one. On the other hand, he did take away what he believed to be the sacred image of Pallas Athena, had it gilded and had it placed in the temple of his own god.

He adopted the religion of the Mother Goddess and went through the ritual of the bull's-blood sacrifice, so that he could steal the image of the goddess and the other sacred objects which are kept hidden. Furthermore, he swaggered about amongst the eunuch priests and tied back his genitalia and did the other things that these castrati do. And when he had taken away the sacred items, he placed them in the shrine of his god. He also celebrated the rites of Salambo with all the frenzied lamentations that you get in that Syrian cult – and in doing so provided an omen for his own imminent doom. In fact he claimed that all gods were the servants of his god, some of them chamberlains, others slaves, still others functionaries of various sorts. He wanted to take away sacred stones from their own temples, and this included removing an image of Diana from its shrine in Laodicea, where Orestes had placed it.

As a matter of fact, Orestes is supposed to have set up an image of Diana not just in the one place, but many of them in different places. After Orestes had purified himself (at the behest of the gods) at Treis Vryses, 'Three Springs,' in the Evros region in Thrace, he founded the city of Oresta (a place that would be stained often with the blood of men), and it was that place, Oresta, that Hadrian ordered to be renamed Adrianople, after *him*. This was at the time when Hadrian began to suffer from delusions, and he, too, was acting at the behest of the gods, because he had been told that he should force his way into a madman's house or a madman's name. He is supposed thereafter to have recovered from the bout of insanity which had caused him to order a large number of senators to be executed. Antoninus Pius saved them, and thus earned his epithet *pius*, 'the Noble', when afterwards he led into the Senate all those thought to have been executed on the emperor's orders.

Heliogabalus also sacrificed human beings, collecting from all over Italy well-born and good-looking boys whose fathers and mothers were alive – I suppose so that the sorrows of bereavement would be that much more if there were two parents. Finally he had around him all kinds of magicians, and had them perform sacrifices every day, urging them on and thanking the gods for being were well-disposed to these men, while he himself was reading the entrails of the children and torturing the victims according to his own rites.

On becoming consul he did not throw silver or gold coins, sweets or miniature animals to the people, but proper cattle, camels, asses and slaves – he said this was more appropriate for an emperor.

He attacked viciously the reputation of Macrinus, but even more so that of Diadumenian, because he had the name Antoninus – he called him a 'Pseudo-Antonine' – and also because he was said to have turned from a complete sybarite into a courageous, honourable, serious-minded and austere man. Moreover, he made some of the chroniclers write (and in a biography, too), improper, or rather, unspeakable things about how profligate he had been.

He established a public bath-house in the palace, and at the same time opened the baths of Plautinus to the public at large, to make it easier for himself to collect numbers of well-hung men. He also went to a lot of trouble to have the whole city, particularly the docks, searched for super-studs – which is the name they gave to men who looked especially virile.

He wanted to make war against the tribe called the Marcomanni, a war that Caracalla had conducted well; some people said that Caracalla had brought about with the help of various sorts of magicians that the Marcomanni tribe would be forever friends and allies of the Romans, and that it had been done with chants and a ritual ceremony. But when Heliogabalus wanted to find out what they were, and where he could get hold of details, he drew a blank. People worked out, in fact, that he was asking about the ritual so that he could destroy it, in the hope of re-starting the war, because he had heard that there was a prophecy that the war with the Marcomanni 'would be ended by Antoninus.' Of course, he was really called Varius and Heliogabalus (not to say 'public laughing-stock'), and only brought the Antonine name, which he had stolen, into disrepute. This story was put about mostly by those who had the misfortune to have as enemies Heliogabalus' well-hung men, the ones well equipped to gratify his lusts. And so people began to think about assassinating him.

This, then, was how he behaved at home.

The soldiers could not stand such a wretch having the imperial title, and they discussed things, first amongst themselves, then in groups, and all turned to Severus Alexander, who had already been named Caesar by the Senate at the time when Macrinus was killed. He was the cousin of our particular Antoninus, because Julia Maesa Varia (from whom Heliogabalus had the name Varius) was grandmother to both of them.

Under the rule of Heliogabalus, a certain Zoticus was given so much importance that he was treated by all the senior officials as if he were the husband of their master Moreover, this man Zoticus was just the type to abuse such a favourable position, and he used to sell under the counter all the words and deeds of Heliogabalus, piling up as much wealth as he could, threatening some of the people, making promises to others, and telling lies to them all. Whenever he came from the emperor, he would go up to people one at a time, and say 'I said this about you, I heard that about you, this is what is going to happen with you . . .' You often get this with men like him – once they have been granted intimate contact with a ruler, they sell information, whether the ruler is good or bad; and either because of stupidity or innocence, the ruler does not see that they are lining their pockets by selling rumours. Heliogabalus went through a form of marriage (even appointing a matron-of-honour), and had sexual relations with Zoticus, shouting, 'stir the pot, cook' – alluding to Zoticus' father. This, in fact, was at a time when Zoticus was ill. Afterwards Heliogabalus used to ask philosophers and men of great seriousness if they, too, had experienced when they were young what he was experiencing, and he did so quite shamelessly; in any case, he never refrained from using dirty words, and he would make rude gestures with his finger while he did so, showing no respect at all, even in public with everybody listening.

He made ordinary freedmen into governors, legates, consuls or generals, and he disgraced every public office by appointing to it some profligate nobody. When he had summoned the senior members of the court to a wine-festival, and had taken his seat by the baskets with the grapes in, he started to ask the most venerable gentlemen whether they could still get it up in bed, and when one of his elderly lordships blushed, he took the silence and embarrassment as a confession, and shouted out: 'he's blushing! It must still be working!' After that he told them what he did himself, without a scrap of shame. And then, when he saw the old men blush and keep silent, inhibited either by age or dignity, he turned to the young men and began to ask them all kinds of things. When he heard from them the sort of things you would expect from men of their age, he got very excited, and said that this was really the way a wine-festival ought to be celebrated. According to a lot of people, he was the first to have jokes told at the expense of senior people (and in their hearing) at wine-festivals, jokes that he himself had composed, mainly in Greek. Marius Maximus records a number of them in his *Life of Heliogabalus*. At his court were a number of depraved types, including old men who looked like philosophers, who had their hair in hair-nets, declared themselves to be perverted, and boasted of having husbands. Some say, however, that they were only pretending, in order to ingratiate themselves more with him by imitating his vices.

As prefect of the Praetorian Guard he appointed a dancer who had been an actor in Rome, he made Gordius the charioteer head of the watch, and put Claudius, a barber, in charge of grain shipments. To the remaining positions of major importance he appointed candidates who commended themselves to him by having enormous penises. He put a muleteer, a courier, a cook and a locksmith in charge of the collection of death-duties. Whenever he went into the Praetorian Camp, or attended the Senate, he took with him the aforementioned Julia Maesa (or Varia), his grandmother, so that he would benefit from her air of authority, since he couldn't command any himself. I have said, too, that before his time no woman had ever attended the Senate to be consulted in the drafting of a bill, or to give a ruling. At banquets he greatly liked to have catamites seated next to him, and he used to enjoy groping and fondling them, and one of them would always pass him his drinking-goblet.

Amongst all the other wicked acts of his shameless life

he ordered that Severus Alexander (whom he had formally adopted) should be removed from him, claiming that he regretted adopting him, and he ordered the Senate to strip him of the title of Caesar. But when this was announced in the Senate there was a profound silence. Severus Alexander was a very fine young man (as became clear later in the way he himself ruled Rome), but was not liked by his adoptive father because he was not profligate. He was, of course, supposedly his cousin, and was popular with the military and accepted by the Senate and the noblity. However, the insane fury of Heiogabalus did not stop at trying to carry out a most wicked plan, and he sent assassins after Alexander in the following manner. Heliogabalus retired to the Spes Vetus Gardens, pretending that he was up to something with a new boyfriend, leaving his mother and grandmother with his cousin in the palace. Then he ordered that Severus Alexander, a noble young man much needed by the state, should be killed. He also sent a written message to the military forces ordering them to strip Severus Alexander of the title of Caesar, and then sent people to smear mud on his title in inscriptions on statues in the Praetorian Camp, which is what is done with despots. Finally he sent word to Alexander's guardians, telling them that if they hoped for any rewards or honours they should kill him in any way they liked – in the bath, by poisoning him, or with the sword.

However, evil men can do nothing against the innocent. No power on earth could induce anyone to carry out such a crime, and the weapons that he was preparing for others would be turned against himself, when he was killed in the way he had in mind for others.

But right after the titles on the statues had been smeared with mud, all the soldiers, now very angry, set out, some of them to the palace, and some to the gardens where Heliogabalus was, so that they could protect Severus Alexander and rid the state at last of this wretched man and would-be murderer. When they reached the palace they put a guard on Alexander, with Julia Mamaea – his own mother – and the grandmother, and then escorted them safely to the Praetorian Camp. Julia Soaemias, the mother of Heliogabalus, followed them on foot, concerned about her son. Then the soldiers went to the gardens, where the emperor was found, making preparations for a chariot race, but really waiting eagerly for someone to report that his cousin had been killed. When he heard the sudden noise of the soldiers, he was terrified, ran in, and hid in a corner, behind the door-curtain of a bedchamber. He sent one of the prefects to the Praetorian Camp to quieten the soldiers, and another to placate those who had just come into the gardens. Antiochianus, one of the prefects of the guard, reminded the soldiers who had come into the garden of the oath of allegiance, and persuaded them not to kill Heliogabalus; in fact not many had come and many were still with the standards, which had been retained by the tribune, Aristomachus. So much for the events in the gardens.

In the Praetorian Camp the soldiers now told the prefect who was trying to placate them that they were prepared to spare Heliogabalus, provided that he would dissociate himself from the dubious characters, charioteers and actors, and return to a decent way of life. Above all, he would have to dismiss those who had, to general dismay, had the greatest influence on him, and who had been making a profit from passing on his words, true or not. And he *did* rid himself of Hierocles, Gordius, a certain Mirissimus, and two other disreputable members of his entourage, who were making him into even more of a fool than he already was. So the soldiers instructed the prefects not to let him keep up the same life-style any longer and to guard Severus Alexander against any acts of violence, and at the same time to prevent him from seeing any of the emperor's friends, in case he might be tempted to imitate their shameful behaviour. Heliogabalus, meanwhile, kept on demanding back that most shameless creature Hierocles, and increased daily his secret plottings against Severus Alexander. Finally, he refused to appear together with his cousin at the ceremony at the beginning of January when they were designated joint consuls, although eventually his mother and grand-mother said that the soldiers were threatening to kill him if they didn't see some signs of harmony between the cousins. So he put on the formal *toga praetexta* and went at mid-day to the Senate, invited his grandmother to the meeting, and escorted her to a seat. But then he refused to go to the Capitol for the swearing-in and conducting of the ceremonies, and everything was done by the urban praetor, as if the consuls were not even in Rome.

Nor did he give up on the murder of his cousin. However, afraid that the Senate might turn to someone else if he did kill Alexander, he suddenly ordered the Senate to leave the city. All of them, even those who had no carriages or slaves were told to set out immediately, some going in litters, others using any animals that they happened to find or could hire. Sabinus, a man of consular rank (to whom Domitius Ulpianus dedicated some of his law-books), stayed in the city, so Heliogabalus called a centurion and told him quietly to kill him. However, the centurion was a little hard of hearing, and thought he had been ordered to expel him, which is what he did. Thus a centurion's deafness proved the saving of Sabinus. The emperor dismissed both Ulpianus himself, the constitutional lawyer, because he was a man of principle, and also Silvinus the rhetorician, whom he had appointed teacher to Severus Alexander. In fact Silvinus was murdered, but Ulpianus was spared.

However, the soldiers, and especially the Praetorian Guard, got up a conspiracy to liberate the state, either because they guessed what fate was being prepared for Heliogabalus, or because they saw his hatred for them. First they killed his associates in his murderous plans in various ways — by disembowelling, or with a spear in the rectum, so that their deaths matched their lives.

After that they went for the emperor, and killed him in a lavatory, where he had hidden. His body was then dragged through the public streets, and as an additional insult to his corpse, the soldiers threw it into a sewer. But since the sewer chanced to be too narrow, the body had weights tied to it to prevent it from floating, and was thrown from the Aemilian Bridge into the Tiber, so that it could never be buried. His body was even dragged around the race-track at the Circus Maximus before it was thrown into the river.

His name, that is, Antoninus, was removed officially by the Senate, because he had held it without any rights, wishing to be seen as the son of Antoninus Caracalla; the names Varius and Heliogabalus were left. After his death he was called 'Son of the Tiber,' 'Dragged-through-the-Streets,' and 'the Unclean One,' as well as many other things which gave a clear indication of what was seen to have been done during his rule. He was the only emperor who was dragged through the streets, dumped in a sewer *and* thrown into the Tiber. This was all because he was generally hated by everybody, something which emperors should be careful to avoid, since they don't earn a decent burial if they haven't earned the love of the populace or the miltary.

There are no remaining examples of any of his public buildings still standing except the temple of the god Elah-Gabal (whom some call the Sun-God, or Jove), the amphitheatre which was restored after the fire, and the baths in the Vicus Sulpicius. These were actually dedicated by Caracalla, who used them himself, and opened them to the public, but there wasn't a portico, and this was added later by our so-called Antoninus; it was completed by Severus Alexander.

Our man was the last of the Antonine emperors (some people think that the Gordians had the surname Antoninus, but it was really *Antonius* that they were called, not *Antoninus*), and his life, habits and profligacy were all so disgusting that the Senate had his name struck from the records. I would myself not have referred to him as Antoninus had it not been for the sake of clarity, which often causes one to use names even when they have been abolished officially.

Julia Soaemias, his mother, was killed at the same time

as he was, a most depraved woman, worthy of such a son. The first thing of all that was done after the fall of Antoninus Heliogabalus was the passing of a decree that no woman should ever enter the Senate, and that anyone who permitted this would be forfeit to the kingdom of the dead.

Many obscene anecdotes about his life have been recorded, but since they are not worthy of being recalled here, I have decided to put down those which relate to his wanton extravagance, some private acts, and some done after he became emperor. He himself said that he wanted to imitate Apicius the gourmet as a private citizen, and Otho and Vitellius as emperors.

He was the first private citizen to cover his couches with a cloth-of-gold, because it had been made legal to do so by Marcus Aurelius, who had sold in public all the imperial trappings. In the summer he gave banquets with a colour-theme – as it might be a green banquet on one day, a glittering one the next, and then a blue one, changing every day throughout the summer. He was the first to have silver cooking-pots and the first to have silver dishes. He also had silver vessels weighing a hundred pounds, some marred by pornographic decorations. He was the first person to spice wine with aromatic gum, or with mint, and to use all the other extravagances that are still with us. He learnt from others about rosé wine, and made it more aromatic with pine-essence. You don't read about drinks of these kinds before Heliogabalus, and indeed, life was to him nothing but a search for sensuous delights. He was the first to make forcemeat out of fish, oysters, clams and other kinds of shellfish, lobsters, crayfish or prawns. He would strew roses and all kinds of other flowers, such as lilies, violets, hyacinths and narcissi, around in his dining-room, couches and portico, and walk about on them. He would not swim in any pool unless it was treated with saffron or some other expensive perfume, nor would he rest easily on cushions unless they were stuffed with rabbit-fur, or partridge-down, and he often changed his pillows.

Frequently he showed contempt for the Senate – he used to call the senators 'slaves in togas' – and he saw the Roman people as the ploughmen of a single farm; the nobility he considered worth nothing. He often invited the urban prefect to drinks after dinner, and also the prefects of the Praetorian Guard, sending a senior official to compel them if they refused to come. He wanted to establish an urban prefect for each of the fourteen districts of Rome, and he would have done so, had he lived, appointing to all the posts men of the worst characters, and the lowest of the low.

He had couches made for his dining-rooms and bed-rooms of solid silver. In imitation of Apicius, he often ate camel-heels, or the combs of living cockerels, or peacocks' tongues or nightingales, because it was said that anyone who ate these was protected against the plague. For his staff in the palace he served up huge plates of red mullet roes, flamingoes' brains, partridge-eggs and thrushes' brains, the heads of parakeets, pheasant and peacock. The beards on the mullets that he ordered were so big, indeed, that he served them like cress, parsely, kidney-beans or fenugreek in full bowls and dishes – it was all absolutely amazing.

He fed his dogs on foie gras, and for pets he kept lions and leopards which had been made harmless and tamed by handlers; at dinner, during the second or third course he would suddenly give them the command to jump up onto the couches, as a joke to scare the wits out of the people who didn't know that they were harmless. He sent expensive Syrian grapes to the stables for his horses, and fed parrots and peacocks to his lions and other beasts. For ten days in a row he served wild sows' udders and wombs – thirty at a time – accompanied by peas and gold pieces, lentils and onyx, beans and amber, and rice with pearls. He sprinkled pearls onto fish and truffles instead of pepper. In a dining room with a reversible ceiling he bombarbed his hangers-on with violets and other flowers to such an extent that some of them suffocated because they could not crawl to the surface. He perfumed his swimming-pools with attar of roses and with wormwood. He invited the ordinary people to drink with him, and drank so much that they thought he was used to drinking from a swimming pool, since he alone could drink such an amount. As gifts at banquets he gave away eunuchs, four-horse chariots, saddle-horses, mules, litters and carriages, and he gave away a thousand gold pieces or a hundred pounds of silver.

At dinners he would give out lucky chances written on spoons, and one might say 'ten camels,' another 'ten flies,' another 'ten pounds of gold' or 'ten pounds of lead,' and yet another 'ten ostriches,' or 'ten hen's eggs.' You really had to trust to chance. He did the same thing at his games, with lots for 'ten bears,' 'ten dormice,' 'ten lettuces' or 'ten gold pieces.' He was the first to introduce this kind of lottery, which we still have. But he also invited paid performers to 'take a chance,' offering dead dogs, or a pound of steak in the lots, or again ten gold pieces or a thousand silver coins, or a hundred copper ones – things like that. This was a crowd-pleaser, and made him a popular emperor after he had done things like that.

He gave a naval display on the canal round the Circus Maximus, having filled it with wine, and he sprinkled everyone's cloak with wild-grape perfume; he drove a chariot with four elephants in the Vatican area, destroying the tombs which were in the way, and he once yoked four camels to a chariot in a private show at the Circus. He is said to have collected serpents with the help of snake-handling shamans from the Marsic people in central Italy, and suddenly to have let them loose before dawn, when people were queuing up for the more popular games; many people were hurt in the panic, or from snakebites. He would wear a tunic entirely of cloth-of-gold, or a purple one, or a Persian costume studded with jewels, of which he used to say that he bore the burden of pleasure on his shoulders. He even had jewels on his shoes, sometimes carved gem-stones; this was a matter of general ridicule, because the engraving-work of famous artists could hardly be seen on gems that he was wearing on his feet. He also wanted to wear a jewelled tiara, to make make himself look more beautiful and his face more like a woman's – and he actually did so at home. It is said that he promised some guests a phoenix, or a thousand pounds of gold instead, and gave this much out in the palace. He set up swimming-pools filled with sea-water a long way inland, and gave them to individual friends to swim in, or he would fill them with fish. One summer he had a mountain of snow (which he had ordered to be brought there) erected in his garden. When by the sea he never ate fish, but in places a long way from the sea he always served all kinds of sea-food. When inland, he used to feed the country people with a soup of sea-eels or dogfish.

He always ate his fish cooked in a blue sauce, as if in sea-water, so that they kept their own colours. He provided for the swimming pools he was using at any given time either attar of roses or actual roses, and when he bathed with all his retinue he provided aromatic oil for the hot-room afterwards, and balsalmic oil for the lamps. He never had sex with the same woman more than once (except his wife), and he provided an in-house brothel for his friends, associates and slaves. He never spent less than a hundred thousand sesterces – thirty pounds of silver – on a dinner, and sometimes it came to three million sesterces, when everything was added in that he had spent. Indeed, he surpassed the dinners given by Vitellius and Apicius. He would take fish from his own stock-pools by the cartload, but in the market place he would express great sorrow for the poverty of the people. He used to tie his hangers-on to a water-wheel, and plunge them into the water, then bring them up again by turning it – calling them 'Ixions-in-the-river.' He used green serpentine and red porphyry underfoot in the courtyards of what he called his Antonine Palace – these paving stones were still there within living memory, but have since been removed and cut up. he planned to set up a huge single column which could have a staircase inside it, and to place the god Elah-Gabal on the top, but he failed to find enough stone, though he was planning to get it from Thebes, in Egypt.

He would often lock his friends in their rooms when they were drunk, and suddenly during the night he would send in his (harmless) lions, leopards and bears, so that when his friends woke up they would find in the bedroom with them at first light – or, what is worse, actually during the night – these lions, leopards or bears; several of the friends died of fright. He used to seat many of his lower-ranking friends on air-filled cushions, and let the air out while they were eating, so that these diners often suddenly found themselves under the table. He also introduced the idea of having people sit not on couches, but in a semi-circle on the floor, so that the serving-boys could let the air out of the cushions with their feet.

Whenever there was a stage performance involving adultery, he ordered that what should have been an imitation was actually the real thing. He often bought prostitutes from all the pimps, and then set them free. Once in a private discussion the question arose of how many men there were in Rome with a hernia, and he ordered them all to be noted and taken to the baths, and he bathed with them himself – and some of them were respectable people. Before banquets he often used to watch gladiatorial fights and boxing-matches. He would spread a couch for himself in an upper gallery, and during the meal would arrange for a wild beast hunt with criminals. He often served his hangers-on with food in their second course made of wax, or wood, or ivory or pottery, and sometimes even of marble or stone, in such a way that all the things he ate himself would be served to them as well, but of different material, so that all they could do was drink with every single course, and then wash their hands as if they *had* eaten.

He was the first man in Rome – it is said – to wear all-silk garments, though garments partly made of silk had been in use before. He never touched washed linen, and said that only beggars wore linen that had been washed. He often appeared in public after dinner wearing a long-sleeved Dalamtian tunic, calling himself 'Fabius Gurges', or 'Scipio', saying that he was wearing the same clothes that the republican consuls Fabius Maximus Gurges or Cornelius Scipio Asiaticus used to wear in their youth, when they were brought out in public by their parents to learn polite behaviour.

He brought together in a public building all the whores from the Circus, the theatre, the stadium and all the baths and public places, and delivered an oration to them like a general addressing his troops, calling them 'comrades-in-arms' and talking to them about different positions and about debauchery. After this he had a similar gathering for procurers, perverts from everywhere, and the most dissolute collection of pretty-boys and young men. When he addressed the whores he had been wearing women's clothes with sticking-out falsies; in front of the perverts he dressed like a rent-boy. After his speech he announced a bounty of three gold pieces each, just as if they were soldiers, and asked them to pray to the gods that they might find others for him.

He also used to play jokes on his slaves by commanding them to bring him a thousand pounds of spiders' webs, and offered a prize; it is said that he collected ten thousand pounds of spiders' webs and then said that it showed how big Rome is! He used to send his hangers-on jars containing frogs, scorpions, snakes and other horrible reptiles of that sort as their annual salaries. He also used to trap vast numbers of flies in jars, and call them 'tame bees.'

He was forever bringing four-in-hand chariots from the Circus into his dining-rooms or entrance-halls while lunching or dining, and made old men (some of whom had held public office) who were dining with him drive them. When he became emperor he used to command people to bring him ten thousand mice, a thousand weasels, or a thousand shrews. He had such good confectioners and dairymen that they could match the different kinds of food that his meat- or fruit-cooks produced, making them as sweets or out of dairy-produce. He served his hangers-on with dinners made of glass, and sometimes he would send to the table decorated napkins on which was depicted whatever food had been placed before him, course for course, so that all that was put before *them* was the product of the embroidery needle or the loom. Sometimes, moreover, painted pictures were shown to them, so that they got, as it were, the whole dinner, whilst being tortured with the pangs of hunger. Heliogabalus would also mix jewels with flowers or fruit, and used to throw as much food out of the window as he served up to his friends. He ordered that an amount of grain equivalent to a year's tribute to the Roman people be given to the whores, pimps and perverts within the walls, and he promised the same to those outside, since at that time, thanks to the foresight of Septimius Severus and of Caracalla, there was the equivalent of a seven years' grain tribute available.

He harnessed four huge dogs to his chariot and drove about the royal palace grounds, and did the same (when still a private citizen) on his country estates. He also appeared in public once driving four massive stags. He harnessed lions, and declared that he was the Great Mother Goddess, or tigers, when he called himself Bacchus – and he used to dress up in the costume in which the god he was imitating was usually painted. In Rome he kept little Egyptian snakes (which are called 'beautiful spirits' in Egypt), as well as hippos, a crocodile, a rhino, and indeed anything from Egypt that could be brought over. He sometimes served ostrich at his dinners, saying that there was a Jewish law that they should be eaten. One really odd thing that he is said to have done was to invite several high-ranking men to dinner, cover a semi-circular dining couch with saffron, and say that he had served up the sort of hay that suited their rank. He carried out daytime activities during the night, and night-time ones during the day; he thought that it was a proper luxury to wake up late, and then receive people, and not go to sleep until the next morning. He received his friends every day and seldom let them go without a present, except for those who were actually thrifty – he reckoned that they were beyond saving!

His carriages were gilded or jewel-encrusted, and he scorned those that were finished in silver, ivory or bronze. He harnessed very beautiful women in fours, in pairs, or even in threes or in greater numbers, to a little dog-cart, and would drive around in it, usually naked, just as the women pulling him were naked. He also had a habit of inviting eight bald men to dinner, or eight one-eyed men, or eight gouty men, eight deaf men, eight dark men, eight tall men, or eight fat men (in which case a single dining couch would not take them all and this would get a laugh from everyone). He would give his guests as presents all the silver plate he had in the dining room, and all the goblets too – and he did this a good few times.

He was the first Roman leader to serve watered fish-sauce in public, a dish known before that only as a soldiers' dish (and to whom Severus Alexander swiftly restored it). He used to propose to his guests, furthermore, as a kind of test, that they should invent new sauces for flavouring, and for the one that pleased him most he gave a large prize, such as a silk garment, which in those days was viewed as a rare honour. But if he didn't like the sauce, he ordered the inventor to go on eating it until he invented a better one. He always sat among flowers or precious perfumes. He also loved to hear people exaggerate the price of food served at his table, and said that this sharpened the appetite at a feast.

He used to make himself up as a confectioner, a perfume-dealer, a cook, a tavern-keeper or a pimp, and he practised these occupations at home all the time. At one dinner he served, on a great number of tables, the heads of six hundred ostriches, so that the brains could be eaten. Occasionally he would give a banquet with twenty-two courses of splendid food, and between courses he and his guests would bathe, and have sex with women; both he and his guests swore solemnly that this voluptuousness was a great delight. Then again, he once celebrated a great dinner at which each individual course was served in order, in the house of a different friend of his, one of whom lived on the Capitoline Hill, another on the Palatine, another between the Quirinal and the Esquiline, one on the Caelian Hill and one beyond the Tiber; each course was eaten in a different house, and they went to all the houses. It was difficult to finish the banquet in a single day doing it that way, and again between courses there was sex and bathing. He always served a course of 'sybariticum,' which is a mixture of oil and fish-sauce, which the Sybarites had invented in the year they all perished. He is said to have established bath-houses in many places, used them once and then had them destroyed, so that he would not use them again. He is supposed to have done the same with houses, military establishments and summer quarters. But these and other things were made up, I believe, by those who wished to belittle Heliogabalus with a view to ingratiating themselves with Severus Alexander.

It is said that he bought a very famous and extremely beautiful whore for a hundred thousand sesterces, and kept her untouched, like a virgin. When someone asked him while he was still a private citizen, 'aren't you afraid of becoming poor,' he is supposed to have answered, 'what could be better than for me to be my own heir and my wife's?' He had plenty of money, and many people left him inheritances because of their regard for Caracalla. He also said that he wanted no sons in case one of them turned out to be thrifty. He ordered that Indian perfumes should be burned without coals so that their odours would fill his rooms. Again, whilst still a private citizen he never went on a journey with fewer than sixty carriages, which caused his grandmother, Julia Maesa, to say that he would waste everything. Once he became emperor, it is said that he took up to six hundred carriages, asserting that the King of Persia travelled with ten thousand camels, and Nero had done so with five hundred carriages. He needed all these vehicles for his great multitude of pimps, madams, whores, perverts and well-hung sexual partners. He always bathed with the women, and treated them with a depilatory, which he applied also to his own beard; indeed, it is shameful to have to admit that he did it together with and at the same time as the women. He used to shave off his partners' pubic hair, wielding the razor himself, and then shaving his beard with it. He would often strew gold and silver dust around the portico when he went out on foot to his horse or carriage, as they do today with golden sand; he used to complain that he could not do so with amber dust.

He never wore the same pair of shoes twice, and is said never to have worn the same ring twice, either. He often tore up expensive garments. Once he took a whale and weighed it, and then sent his friends what was reckoned to be its weight in fish. He sank some laden ships in the harbour, and said that this showed his great magnanimity. He emptied his bowels in a golden pot and urinated in vessels made of fluorspar. He is also supposed to have said: 'If I have an heir I shall provide him with a tutor who will make him behave as I have done and as I propose to go on doing.' He made a habit of having dinners served to him of a specific kind; one day he would only eat pheasant, and at every course pheasant-meat would be served, another day chicken, another day fish of some kind or other, pork another day, and on another ostrich, or vegetables, or apples, sweets or dairy produce. He often used to lock his friends in overnight rest-houses until morning with ancient Ethiopian women, saying that the women who worked there were said to be the most beautiful. He did the same thing with boys as well, but this was allowed at that time, before the prohibition imposed by Philip I. He used to laugh so loudly that sometimes he was the only one who could be heard in the public theatre. He himself sang, danced, played the pan-pipes, blew the trumpet and played the lute and the pipe-organ. It is said that on one day he visited every whore in the Circus, the theatre, the amphitheatre and all the public places, hidden by a muleteer's hood, so that he would not be recognized, but giving them each a gold piece without making use of them sexually, saying: 'Don't tell a soul, but Antoninus is giving you this.'

He invented several new kinds of licentious behaviour, which went beyond the group-perversions of the old, wicked emperors, and he was well acquainted with what was done by Tiberius, Caligula and Nero.

It had been predicted by a Syrian priest that he would die violently. Therefore he prepared ropes of wound purple and scarlet silk, so that if necessary he could hang himself. He got golden swords ready to stab himself if violently attacked. He prepared, too, poisons hidden in onyxes, amethysts and emeralds with which to kill himself if in danger. He also built a very high tower with golden and jewelled slabs beneath it, from which he could throw himself, saying that even his death should be a rich and luxurious one, and so that it might be said that no-one else had died like that. But it was all to no avail. As already mentioned, he was killed by ordinary soldiers, dragged through the streets, dumped unceremoniously into sewers and thrown into the Tiber.

This was the end the Antonines in public life, though everyone knew that with this Antoninus the name was as false as he was.

It may perhaps appear strange to some people, most worshipful Constantine, that the scourge I have been describing had the position of emperor, and for nearly three years, too. But the state had nobody who could remove him from the government of mighty Rome, where in the cases of Nero, Vitellius, Caligula and others of their sort there had been someone ready to kill the tyrant. But first of all let me apologise for having put down things I found in various writers; I have been silent on many unworthy details, and things that I absolutely could not say without blushing. Indeed, what I *have* said I have tried as best I could to express in oblique terms. Furthermore I have always believed that we should consider your own words, your Excellency: 'It is Fate that makes a man emperor.' There have indeed been less good rulers, and also extremely bad ones. And as you, most pious sir, are accustomed to say, we have to make sure that those whom the force of fate has made emperor are worthy of it. And since Heliogabalus was the last of the Antonines, and no-one else of this name ruled the state after this, something must be added, to prevent any misunderstanding when I start to tell the stories of the two Gordians, father and son, who wanted to be named after the Antonine family. First, they did not have the family name but only the fore-name, and secondly I find in many books that they were called Antonius rather than Antoninus.

That, then, was Heliogabalus, whose life-story you wanted, a story which I (somewhat reluctantly and unenthusiastically) researched in Greek and Latin texts, to write and offer to you, having already done so with earlier emperors. I shall now begin to write about those who came afterwards, of whom Severus Alexander was the best, worth writing about in detail; he ruled for thirteen years, where the others had six months, or at best a year or two. Aurelian was the most distinguished, but the glory of them all was Claudius Gothicus, founder of your line. I am somewhat afraid to write about this man to Your Excellency, in case I appear to my ill-wishers to be a flatterer. But I shall be absolved of any charges laid by envious and evil people because plenty of others have seen him as a fine man. To these we must add Diocletian, father of the golden age, and Maximianus, father (as is commonly said) of the age of iron, as well as the rest down to yourself, most noble sir. You yourself, most revered emperor, shall be described in many more eloquent pages by those to whom kind fate has granted this. We shall have to add Licinius, Valerius Severus, Domitius Alexander and Maxentius, all of whose power gave way to yours, but I shall write of them in such as way as not to play down their strengths. For I have no intention of doing what many writers do, and belittle the achievements of those who have been defeated; it will enhance your glory, if I tell the truth about all their merits.

Juvenal

Satire VI

Juvenal's famous diatribe against the women of his day.

VI

In the remotest past I think that chastity
could still be found on earth – when men lived in cold caves
or when they had their fires and their household gods,
the livestock and their owners all under one roof.
Their country-bred wives from the forests or the hills
would make their beds from straw or skins of savage beasts
– quite different from *you*, dear Cynthia, or you,
still weeping for that sparrow, Lesbia my love! –
their breasts provided milk for robust infants, who
were often shaggier than their acorn-grubbing men.
Back in those days, the heavens and the earth were new,
and men lived then hewn out of oak-trees, fully formed,
or moulded (with no parents of their own) from earth.
It may be that some traces of this chastity
survived, but only in the Golden Age on earth,
(before the Greeks got devious, or people lived
in fear of theft), when folk still left their gates unlocked.
Just after that the last immortal fled the world,
and took her sister, Chastity, away with her.
But now, my friend, the habit's well established to
bounce on the springs of other people's marriage-beds.
All other sins came later, in the Age of Iron,
but not adultery – that came much earlier.

But what's all this? You've got engaged and called the
banns, and in *this* day and age! You've had a haircut, too,
you've even been and bought a wedding ring! My friend,
you used to be quite sane, and now you're getting wed?
Has someone cast a spell, or something bitten you,

that you'll submit yourself to domination from
some woman, when there's rope, or windows you could
use, or bridges you could jump off to your doom? Or if
none of these tested methods turns you on, then get
yourself a pretty little rent-boy for your bed –
a pretty boy won't bitch at you for half the night,
won't be forever begging little gifts, and won't
complain that you don't match up to his bedtime needs.

But no! Our former wild-oats-man now praises
the marriage-laws, wants kids, is happy to forgo
fat pigeons, bearded mullet – all the stuff like that.
If *he's* prepared to take a wife, then anything
is possible – when this guy, randiest of all
the rams, gives up, accepts the wedding ball-and-chain –
a man who used to hide in wardrobes all the time!

And all this searching for a sweet, old-fashioned girl!
(Doctors – make sure he takes his little yellow pills!)
You're mad! You'd have to make a massive sacrifice
to Juno (say, a calf with horns of purest gold)
if you should find a wife who's modest and who's chaste.
You don't find all that many who could wed in white,
or who the father would be proud to give away.
O.K., deck out your house with orange-blossom
wreaths, but will she ever be content with just *one* man?
She'd be more likely to forfeit one of her eyes!

So, there's this girl who lives out on her papa's farm,
and she's still pure? Well, let her come and spend some
time in any town you like – then I'll believe it's true!
Besides, who says it can't be done on hills, or in
dark caves? And Mars and Jupiter aren't past it yet!

Is there a woman worthy of these vows in any

shopping mall? And the theatres – try and find
one woman in those many seats that you could love.
Some long-haired singer's writhing on the stage, and
makes one wee girl wet herself, another give a moan
of ecstasy, as if she'd suddenly been done –
and back-woods girls are very quick to learn the score!

Others again, when all the theatres are dark,
and everything is shut except the law-courts, and
it's still a long while till September, ease the pain
of boredom by a lively interest in the arts.
In bedroom farces, Urbicus gets all the laughs,
and Aelia is hot for him (and now she's broke).
Others, who've got the cash, can rent-a-Thespian,
but don't want elocution lessons. One of them
likes tragic actors (scholars wouldn't stand a chance!).

Go on and take a wife! And let some musician
– a drummer or guitarist – do some fathering!
Then you can throw a party for the christening,
lay on a spread, and generally celebrate
that in his little cradle, sonny-boy will look
just like that singer, or that boxer – but not *you*.

When Eppia, the politician's wife, ran off
to Egypt with a gladiator, Africa
itself condemned the shameful morals here in Rome.
Forgetting husband, home and family, she left
her weeping children and ignored her fatherland,
and (odder still) the race-track and her favourite star.
Although she started with a silver spoon, and slept
on eiderdown while she was in the cradle, she
scoffed at the waves and at her reputation, too,
(though that's not something our dear ladies mind about).
And so she braved the roaring Tyrrhenian Sea,
and the Ionian, without a qualm, and then
the many other seas she had to cross. When honest

215

dangers threaten, then a woman's heart will freeze
with fear, she trembles so that she can hardly stand.
But if she up to wickedness, then she'll not quail!
She won't take ship on orders from her husband, it's
unfair — she's seasick and the skies spin round and round.
But if she's following a lover, then she's fine —
it's hubby who gets puked on. Cheerfully she joins
the sailors, roams the decks and hauls upon the ropes.

What did he have to offer, Eppia's young man?
What turned her on, till she was called a 'gladiator's
moll?' Her darling Sergius was no smooth-faced lad,
a wound would soon have got his discharge from the ring,
and anyway, he was an ugly specimen,
with helmet-scars, and on the middle of his nose
an ugly mole, and one eye permanently wept.
But then, he *was* a fighter. That's what does the trick,
that's what displaces country, husband, sisters, kids.
The ladies love a gladiator's sword. Discharge
our Sergius and you'll see his interest-level fall.

Why should a commoner like Eppia bother us?

Well, what about our god-like monarchy, and what
old Claudius put up with? When his wife saw that
he was asleep, that harlot-on-the-throne
exchanged his noble bedroom for a knocking-shop.
She'd leave the palace, hooded and with just one maid,
her black hair hidden underneath a long blonde wig,
and go down to some smelly whore-house in the town,
straight to the cubicle they kept for her. With gold-
tipped tits exposed ('Lycisca' was her working name),
she'd bare the belly that bore young Britannicus!
She coolly took on every punter (and his fee),
she'd just lie back and take the bonking as it comes.
But when the pimp called time and paid the girls, she'd
wait until the very end, and only sadly close

her pitch, her fanny hot and gasping for some more,
and off she went, shagged out, but still not satisfied,
all grimy from the smoky little lamp, and took
the fetid brothel-smell back to her palace bed.

Why should we talk of potions, charms, or things slipped
in a stepson's drink? The ladies go in for worse crimes
when driven on by sex; but lust's the least of it.

Why does her husband call Censennia 'the best
of wives?' She brought him millions! *That's* why she's
'chaste.'
It wasn't cupid's darts that lit his fire, it was
her dowry turned him on! And all that cash brought her
her freedom. She can write what billets-doux she likes,
a woman married for her dowry's off the hook.

Why does Sertorius burn with desire for his
wife, Bibula? It's not his wife, it's just her face
he loves. But when the wrinkles come, or flabby skin,
or dodgy teeth, or eyes that lose their shine, then that's
her lot! 'Get packed,' the word will be, 'and on your way!
You've turned into a sniffling drag, so – on your way!'
and 'your replacement won't be sniffling all the time.'
Meantime, however, she's still in complete control,
demanding livestock, shepherds, vineyards, vines and
wines.
You think that's all? His slaves, too, boys *and* older ones;
and anything the neighbours have, she makes him buy.
And in December, when the winter market's in
full swing, and every kind of stall sets out its wares,
she'll buy great crystal vases, and then bigger ones
of agate; *then* she'll buy a diamond ring once worn
by Berenikè, the Judaean queen, who got
it from Agrippa, barbarous sister-loving king
of that strange land of curious sabbath rituals,
and where the pigs (that no-one eats) die of old age.

And still there's no-one you would wed in all that lot?

Let's say you find a pretty, rich and fecund wife,
with pedigree a mile long, and twice as chaste
as all those Sabine women who once stopped the war
(admittedly as rare a bird as – say – a coal-black swan),
yet – who could bear a wife perfect in all respects?
I'd rather wed a barmaid than a duchess, if
she's so damned supercilious that she includes
among the dowry that she brings the marriage, all
the battle honours that her brave ancestors won,
as far back even as the Punic Wars! No, thanks!

'I beg of you, Apollo, please, Diana – spare
my children, for it is their mother who has sinned!'

Thus prayed Amphion. But Apollo killed them all,
and slew their father too, because Niobe said
that she was better bred than Leto (mother of
the god and goddess), and she was more fertile, too.

However beautiful, is any wife worth while
who always puts you down? Her aristocracy
is useless if she's filled so full of pride
it leaves a nasty taste. And no-one's *ever* been
that much besotted that, for half the time, at least,
he wouldn't try hard to avoid his much-praised wife.

It's little things, of course, that husbands cannot bear.
What, for example, would be worse than when a wife's
not satisfied to look Italian, but wants
to be a Greek, not Tuscan but Athenian?
It's Greek, Greek, Greek (although her Latin's terrible!).
They worry, moan, rejoice and vent their spleen in Greek,
pour out the deepest secrets of their souls – in Greek,
and – yes – they love in Greek. It's O.K. in a girl,
but all you older ladies now – why keep it up?
It's so indecent! Mucky phrases like *zoè*

kai psychè, 'O, my life, my soul' – it's bedroom talk
in public! These are words that go straight for the crotch
like fingers! Even if your voice is sweet and low
and you can put it over like an actress, it
won't have the right effect – you're just too bloody *old*!

Now, if you don't propose to love your legally
betrothed and wedded wife, there seems to be no cause
to wed, nor pay for wedding-breakfast, cake, and all
those farewell gifts for parting guests, nor what you have
to give *her* as a present – say, a silver dish
inlaid with costly gold, and beautifully engraved.
But if you *are* uxorious, devoted to
one woman, then just bow down and accept the yoke.
You'll never find a woman who will spare the man
who loves her; even if she loves him back, she'll still
torment and rob him. And the better a man is,
his wife will be proportionately bad for him.

You can't give anyone a gift unless she says
you may, nor buy or sell a thing without her full
approval. And she'll pick your friends – turn old ones from
your door, although you've known them since you were
at school.
The meanest pimp can leave his goods to whom he likes,
and so can gladiators and their trainers, too;
but you'll be made to name your rivals in your will.

'Have that slave crucified!' 'Why? What has he done
wrong?
Where are the witnesses? Who brought the charge? Hear
him!
You can't spend too much time when a man's life's at
stake.'
'You fool, he's not a man, he's just a slave. And if
he's innocent, so what? *I* want it – that's enough.'
And so she rules the roost. But not for very long.

She changes homes and wedding-dresses frequently,
and sometimes tries a marriage bed a second time,
leaving the newly-decorated hearth and home
with remnants of the wedding-breakfast still around,
to keep the score of husbands up – it's *eight* so far,
in just five years!
I bet they'll write that on her tomb!

Your new mother-in-law will make sure that you get
no peace. It's she who'll teach your wife to rob you with
a smile. She teaches her to answer lovers' notes
with subtlety and style, not innocence; she bribes
your guards, or gets around them; she's the one who'll call
the doctor when there's nothing wrong, so your wife stays
in bed – and all the while her lover waits and hides
in silent eagerness, with one hand on his cock.
You don't expect Mama to teach her decency,
or habits different from her own? The odious
old slag will find it useful if her girl is ghastly, too.

Cherchez la femme in every case in every court!
Some woman's always either plaintiff or defence.
She'll be in firm control, she'll sort out all the briefs,
and tell the counsel how to open, plead, or close.

We've all seen women athletes in their red tracksuits,
those lady wrestlers or fencers, in the gym,
hacking and thrusting, training with their swords and
shields, and doing all the things a swordsman does.
It's one thing playing fanfares at the games – but no,
she wants to go to the arena for a fight!
How modest can a woman be who wears a helmet,
in defiance of her sex, loves violence,
but doesn't want to *be* a man (she'd miss too much)?
And what if you were selling off your wife's effects
and had to sell her . . . *studded belt?* her *gauntlets and
knee-pads?* Or, if she'd been a gladiator-ess

think how you'd love to sell her weaponry!
And yet these darling creatures find chiffon too hot,
their delicacy sweats and frets in sheerest silk.
Just look at how she pants and trembles with each thrust,
and how the helmet weighs her down, how big and rough
the padding she wraps round her thighs! You have to
laugh, though, when she takes a break, and has to squat to pee!
Tell us, you noble ladies, all descended from
the great men of the past, what gladiator's wife
would ever once have dressed or played with swords like
that?

There's always argument and bitching in a bed
that has a wife in it – no chance of any sleep.
She sets upon her husband like a tigress that
has lost her young – but worse! Although she's far from
pure she'll whinge about the girls – or boys – she says he's had.
She keeps a good supply of tears ready for use
in any way she needs – she simply lets them flow.

And you, poor sap, believe in every single tear,
and kiss them all away. But what love-letters you
might find in your adulterous wife's locked writing-case!
Or you might find her in some noble lover's arms;
'quick, Cicero,' she'll say, 'I need some rhetoric!'
'No chance! You're on your own!'
'Well then,' she says . . . 'Ah, yes.
Surely we once agreed that each of us would do
our own thing? You can scream from now till doomsday,
but I need my personal space!'
There's no cheek like a woman's
caught red-handed, covering her guilt with rage.

But where do all these dreadful things come from, you
ask.

Back in the old days, poverty kept women chaste,
hard work and little sleep kept vice away, their hands
hardened by waulking, in the days when Hannibal
besieged the gates, and all their husbands were in arms.
But now we're suffering from a peace that's been too
long.
High living, worse than enemies, takes vengeance for
the world we conquered. We've tried every sin or crime
since Rome stopped being poor but chaste. That was the
time when sybarism just came flooding in upon
our seven hills, in wild Dionysian lust!
Cash-grubbing brought in filthy foreign ways to Rome,
while wealth corrupted all of us and made us soft.

Has Venus any conscience when she's drunk? Or when
she can't tell head from fanny, when at midnight in
some *chambre separée* she's scoffing oysters and
champagne, till all the room is spinning round and round,
the table's dancing and she sees everything twice?

O.K., what does that sniffy Tullia say to her
pal Maura (who's notorious), when they pass the old
and noble altar of the Goddess Chastity?
It's here at night they get out of their litters for
a pee, and treat the goddess to a mighty stream,
then finger one another while the moon looks down,
and then go home. I bet next day you'll tread, when off
to see important people, in your own wife's piss.

And everybody knows the secrets of the Great
Goddess, whose flute incites the drunken, frenzied loins
of howling worshippers of the priapic god.
The only thought they have is that of being screwed,
they screech in leaping lustfulness, and all the while
the ancient juices flow in torrents down their thighs.
Saufeia challenges the call-girls to a match,
and she can move her pelvis with the best, but even

she admires the wiggling of Medullina's
bum — pride of them all! She's really born to it!
None of this stuff is simulated, mind! It's all
quite real, and it would warm the blood (and tease the
balls) of superannuated Nestor, or Priam.
Delay just makes them hot for it, raw females now,
they shout and cry from everywhere, 'it's time, it's time!
we're ready, just bring on the men!' If one's asleep,
they'll hurry up and drag another out instead.
If men run out, they'll use the slaves. If that's no good,
they'll pay the water-carrier to come in. And if
they can't find *any* men, they'll just as soon raise up
their bottoms to a donkey as a substitute.
Sad, that our ancient practices (or public rites
at least) are desecrated by this wickedness.

But everybody in the wide world knows the so-
called 'lady harpist,' who took in a prick longer
by far than Caesar's speeches, to the shrine where all
male images have to be covered, where a mouse,
if male, is shamed even by tiny testicles.
Who ever would have mocked the gods in days gone by,
or would have laughed at the (albeit crude, but sacred)
vessels used back then? Nobody would have dared!
But every altar seems to be profaned today.

Ogulnia dresses to the nines to see the games,
spends cash on her attendants, friends, a litter and
a little fair-haired girl to come and go for her.
And still she'll give the last bits of the family
silver to some young athlete, plates and cups and all.
These women often aren't well-off, but poverty
has taught them nothing about shame, nor how to live
within their means. It's always different with men —
they have an eye for practicality; the ant's
example teaches them to fear the cold and hunger,
while a wasteful woman never knows just what

she's spent; and just as if she thought it grew on trees,
or if her money maybe multiplied itself,
she never gives a thought to what her pleasures cost.

In every house where just one person is corrupt
and studiedly obscene (his twitching right hand says
it all), you'll find he brings in other dirty types,
and they'll pollute your very crockery for you
(better to smash it after them, than try to clean
the cups and plates *these* characters have used!)

In fact, a gladiator-trainer's house is better-run
than yours. *He* separates the straight ones from the not-
so-straight, and keeps the ex-cons from the rest. Nor will
you find that different kinds of gladiators (like
a swordsman and a net-and-trident fighter) share
a cell. The very lowest of the low are kept
chained up together, like with like, when they're in jail.
But your wife makes you drink from the same cup as folk
with whom the cheapest whore (who gives knee-tremblers in
the graveyard) wouldn't drink, however good the wine.
But they advise on marriage (or when to withdraw),
their chattering relieves her jaded soul, and they
teach her to bump and grind (they're very good at that),
plus many other tricks. However – do not trust
that teacher! Yes, I know he paints his eyes, and likes
to wear a frock, but it's adultery that's on
his mind. Just watch out for that pansy voice, and for
the way he minces up and down, his wrist all limp –
he's really a terrific stud! Once in her room
he'll drop the doe-eyed bit, and be a rutting stag!
I'd say: 'Come on, mate, try it, but you don't fool
me! I know that you're all man.' I'd say: 'Own up!
Confess, or else we'll torture it out of your maids.'

I know exactly what my friends would say. 'Lock up

your wife, and keep her well indoors.' But who will guard
the guardians? They'll be well paid (the usual way)
for keeping quiet on the lady's (and their) sins.
Of course, a crafty wife's bound to sort them out first!
A woman's lust is just the same if she is high
or low, whether she has to walk the pavement with
bare feet, or ride a litter, every one's the same.

Now some girls like a soft and gentle eunuch best,
and love to kiss those ever-beardless cheeks. Of course,
that way, abortion's never even on the cards.
Their greatest lust's for one who was mature before
the doctors got into his black and hairy groin!
You see, they wait until the testicles both grow
and drop, until they weigh a kilogramme apiece,
then snip! But it's only the barber who'll complain.
Those eastern lads you buy don't have such quality –
the things that *they* had chopped were only peanut-sized.

That chap, now, – highly visible, well-known to all,
you wouldn't doubt his strength when he shows off,
down at the baths! And yet his mistress had him spayed. He
sleeps with her, though, and I bet it would be hard to find
a smooth (but fully-fitted) lad to do as well.

If she likes music, no professional singer
will ever get away from her. An instrument
is always in her hands, they flash over her lute,
rings glittering. She plays arpeggios so well,
and keeps her fingers tight around the plectrum, which
she loves so much – just look at how she kisses it!

There was a famous titled lady once, who spent
a fortune sacrificing to all of the gods
so that her favourite guitarist had a chance
to carry off some prize. It might have been expected

if her husband had been ill, or if her son
were dying. Standing by the altar, without shame,
head veiled, she offered up the proper prayers – for some
strummer! And paled, when they took the auguries.
Tell me, O Father Janus, oldest of the gods,
do you give answers to a prayer like that? I know
time's on your hands – up there there's nothing else to do.
One lady's prayers are for a comic, one for a
tragedian – the augur's feet are killing him!

Better a music-freak, though, than a wife who runs
around the city, bold as brass, meeting with men,
with brazen face and shrivelled tits, talking to four-
star generals, while her wretched husband's looking on.
She's always well-up on the international news,
what the Chinese are up to, or the Greeks, and who
is screwing whom, and who's the latest super-stud;
she'll say who put that widow in the club (and when);
she'll tell you what each woman says in bed (and how).
If things are getting sticky in Armenia,
she'll be the first to know; she picks up rumours in
the street – or *makes* them up: like how some river's burst
it's banks and drowned the local populace, or that
an earthquake's bringing lands and cities down; she'll rush
about and make sure everyone has heard the 'news.'

No less intolerable is a woman who
loses her temper with her poorer neighbours,
and sets about them; if their barking dogs should wake
her up at night, it's 'quick, a stick!' and then she'll say
'go over there and thrash the owner, then the dog!'
You wouldn't want to meet her sort – and what a face!
She goes down to the baths at evening, takes her oils
and soaps and all her stuff, and then enjoys the throng,
and when her arms are tired out from pumping weights,
she'll let the masseur's clever fingers do their work
along her thighs, right up, until she gasps and cries!

*

Meanwhile her house-guests, bored and hungry, wait
around till she comes in, red-faced and with a thirst
enough to sink the massive jug of first-class wine that's
put in front of her, and then she'll take another pint
or two before she eats, to work an appetite –
and *then* she spews the lot, so that it floods the room,
and pours in streams over the marble floor. She pukes
on golden dishes, drinks and spews like some great snake
that's fallen in a wine-vat. All the while, to keep
his own bile down, her sickened husband shuts his eyes.

But worse again's the woman who, when she sits down
to dine, starts praising Vergil, justifies Dido,
and starts comparing poets, takes Vergil and sets
Homer against him, weighing and contrasting them.
The critics all give up, dons are defeated, and
they all shut up – nobody gets a single word
in edgeways, man or woman. She talks such a lot,
you think of saucepans clashing, or of gongs,
No need for trumpets and no need for magic drums,
one woman's noise will frighten evil spirits off!
She dishes out opinions till the cows come home,
wanting to seem both wise and eloquent;
she should be wearing trousers and a scholar's gown,
or she should go and join some club for gentlemen.
Don't pick a wife who's over-fond of rhetoric,
and practices by hurling shafts of wit at you
in flowery style, and knows the whole of history.
No, let there be things in her books that she *can't* grasp.
I hate these women who are walking grammar-books,
observing every single rule and law of speech
and quoting, like some ancient don, from books that no-
one's read. She *will* correct her dimmer women-friends;
at least let *husbands* make grammatical mistakes!

There's nothing that a woman won't allow herself,
nor counts as shame – not when she puts those emeralds

around her neck, or weighs her earlobes down with pearls.

A wealthy woman?
I can think of nothing worse!
Sometimes she looks ridiculous, a face-pack made
of soggy bread slapped on, or plastered with some cream
so greasy her poor husband's lips stick fast to it.
For lovers, she will wash, but why should she look nice
at home? She only buys expensive foreign scent
(brought in from India) for some lover's benefit.

So gradually we get to recognise her face
as layers of junk are cleaned away with asses milk
(for which she'll need to take a herd of she-asses
as luggage if they ever have to move up north).
But when she's slapping creams and lotions all over
her skin, and when she's got that doughy face-pack on –
well? has she got a face at all, or just a boil?

It's worth the effort to try and find out just what
these ladies *do* all day.
Let's say, last night in bed
her husband turned his back on her. God help the staff! –
she'll flay her manicurist, curse her driver for
his idleness (though hubby was the sleepy one).
One slave will get a flogging till the birches break,
others get rods or whips (floggers are kept in work).

And while they're flogged, she'll do her face, listen and
chat to friends, or look at some posh dress-material,
(lash! lash!) and then she'll read the paper to the end,
(lash! lash!) until the floggers are exhausted and
the nasty deeds are done, and she snarls 'off with you.'

She runs her home like some totalitarian state.
If she should have an assignation, and should want
to look her best (her lover's in the garden, or

more likely by the temple – brothel? – of Isis),
she'll tear her hairdresser's own hair out, rip her clothes
right off the breast and shoulder of the wretched girl.
'These curls ought to be tighter!' So down comes the lash
hard, as a punishment for the offending lock.
Why was the girl to blame? How could it be her fault
if you dislike your nose's shape? Another maid
back-combs and curls the hair on her left side. One of
her mother's women (once a seamstress, now looking
after the linen) offers her expert advice.
She's first, then other lesser mortals all join in,
as if some point of life or honour were at stake.
She takes this beauty-treatment oh-so-seriously;
her hair is piled in layers high upon her head,
so from the front she looks just like some giantess,
but from behind she's shorter –is this someone new?
It's worse if she is on the short side anyway,
no bigger than a pigmy (when not wearing heels),
and has to stand on tip-toe if she wants a kiss.
But anyway, her husband's never mentioned, nor
how much she costs him; she's more like a neighbour than
a wife, except she hates his friends and all his slaves
but not his bank-book.

       Here's another woman, though,
and she admits a frenzied crowd of worshippers
of Cybele, attended by a huge eunuch
to whom the others pay obscene homage. He chopped
his balls away long since, and now outshrieks the noise
of cymbals, with a diadem on his plebeian
head. He tells the lady grandly to beware
the autumn winds, and orders her to offer up
one hundred eggs, and give to him some russet robes
so that any forthcoming ills can pass into
the clothes – sufficient expiation for a year.
In winter she will break the river's ice, and plunge
three times into the icy Tiber, trembling as
her head goes under swirling waters. Naked and

still shivering, she crawls on bloody knees across
the Field of Mars. If Isis orders her, she'll go
to Egypt, where she'll seek the holy sanctuary
of Meroë, and there she'll fetch the waters back
to sprinkle over Isis' temple here in Rome.
It's her belief the goddess Isis told her to.
(Oh yes, I'm sure the gods chat with *her* sort each night!)
The major honours go to Anubis, the god
whose shaven-headed priests run all around, and mock
in ritual those weeping for Osiris dead.
It's he who pardons wives who fail to abstain
from intercourse on holy days, and he exacts
the fines for violation of the marriage bed,
or when the Silver Serpent's seen to move its head.
His tears and clever mutterings will make quite sure
that Great Osiris grants forgiveness (for a bribe,
of course, a fattened goose, a sacrificial cake).

Once he has left, a twitching Jewess shuffles in
(leaving her gear outside), and softly begs for alms.
She can interpret Jewish laws, she's high priestess
of wanderers, and heaven's mouthpiece here on earth.
She fills her hands, but modestly. Just cross her palm
with copper – Jews will sell you any dream you like.

You'll get a promise of a lover, or a fat
inheritance from someone rich, if once you let
a soothsayer from Armenia dissect a dove;
he'll look into a chicken's heart, a puppy's guts,
– even a boy's (sometimes he'll shop his customers).

Chaldeans – *they* get trusted even more! The words
of these soothsayers are thought to come from Am-un's
Well in Thebes (now that the Delphic oracle is dumb,
the human race cannot know what the future holds).
The greatest, Ptolemy, was often in exile.
His friendship and his prophecies led to the death

of noble Galba, whom Otho had feared so much.
No-one believes a soothsayer unless he's done a spell
in prison, all chained up, and in some distant place.
No-one believes that an astrologer is good
unless he's just dodged execution, or has been
an exile on some island, from which he escaped.

Your lady wife consults them on the reason why
her ailing mother takes so long a-dying, or
why *you* do; when her uncle or her sister's due
to go; or will her lover outlive her (she hopes!).
And yet she doesn't understand the gloomy threats
of Saturn, or when Venus is ascending,
which months are good for money-making, and which
not.

But mind you keep away from any woman who
clutches a well-thumbed almanac, and fiddles with it
all the time; she doesn't seek out fortune tellers,
she *is* one. If her husband's off abroad, or *en
route* home, she'll not go with him if 'the signs are wrong.'
The smallest trip she makes (even a mile), she'll look
up an auspicious hour; she won't put ointment on
an itchy spot without casting her horoscope;
if she is ill in bed, then she won't eat except
at times worked out from her *Egyptian Fortune-Book.*

Less well-off women wander round the fairground
booths at the race-track, to get their fortunes told. They'll
have their bumps felt or their palms read, and they lap it
up! Ric women buy their answers from some Indian
guru who knows the movements of the stars, or from
one of the ancients who can ward off thunderbolts.
Plebeians learn their fortunes at the fair, or on
the street – the low-cut-dress-and-ankle-chain brigade
come for advice: should they chuck out the guy who

runs the bar, and wed the fellow with the old-clothes stall?

At least the women of the lower class put up
with childbirth, and the suffering that nursing brings.
There aren't too many children born in golden beds –
there's too much know-how and too many drugs that
bring about sterility, or help abortionists to kill the unborn
child.
But never mind!
Give her that 'drink' yourself! If she were willing to get fat
and have her womb disturbed with bouncing brats, maybe
you'd find your son was black! An heir who can't be
yours – and you don't want to see – inherits all your cash!

Let us pass over spurious children, foundlings left
on doorsteps, who are cheerfully then introduced
by fate into the finest families in the land.
Dame Fortune hangs about at night quite shamelessly
and smiles down on these naked babes, and takes them all
into her ample bosom; then slips them into
the houses of the great (a little joke of hers).
She loves them. They can count on Fortune all their lives.

This man sells magic charms, and this one potions from
abroad, with which a wife may twist a husband's mind,
so she can kick his butt! If you act oddly, or
get blackouts, or you find your short-term memory's
gone – well then, that's why! But even that's not quite as bad
as being sent completely off your head, as was
Caligula, when his Caesonia spiked his drink
with happy-juice. Well, royal wives always set trends.
But still it put the whole world out of joint, no less
than if Juno had sent her Jupiter insane.
That mushroom Agrippina fed to Claudius
was really not so bad – it only sent one daft

and dribbling, twitching man off to the other world
a little in advance. Caesonia's magic drink
brought with it steel and fire, and torturing – the deaths
in blood of noblemen and senators alike;
and all from just one drink, one single poisoner.

Wives hate the offspring of a mistress. And why not?
Stepsons get murdered all the time, and no-one minds.
But listen – if you've been adopted into wealth,
watch out, especially with what you get to eat!
Those pies that mother made contain a lethal sauce;
if *she* cooked it, make sure that someone else takes the
first bite, and let your trembling tutor try your drinks.

You think it's all made up? That my satire, perhaps
has gone over the top, broken the rules, and wants
to be a Sophoclean tragedy, with themes
appropriate to ancient Greece, but not to Rome?
If only!
Here's a lady not too long ago:
'I did it, I confess, I gave wolfbane to both
my children. Poisoned, certainly! And I did it!'
'Two children at one meal, you wicked viper, *two*
children?' 'If I'd had seven, seven I'd have killed.'

So let's believe in all those ancient tragic tales
of Procne or Medea. Why not? Those women were
most wicked monsters in their day. And yet they did
not kill for gold. Such evil doesn't seem so bad
in women, when it's fury that makes them commit
a crime, or burning rage sweeps them along, just like
a rock that's torn down from a mountain side, falls, and
brings in its wake the hurtling, fatal avalanche.

The very worst are women who plan out great crimes
cold-bloodedly. In plays, our wives watch Alcestis,
prepared to die to save her husband. They would let
their husbands go to save a puppy-dog instead.

You'll often meet those husband-killers from the past –
a Clytemnaestra can be found in every street.
The only difference is, *she* wielded in her hands
the ancient double-headed axe. But nowadays
a little scrap of reptile-venom will suffice.
But maybe cold steel will be needed after all,
if people fortify themselves with antidotes.

THE ACTS OF THE APOSTATES – Geoffrey Farrington

'His was the most monstrous crime a man could commit. In this land it was an act of desecration without parallel.'

In the last days of the Emperor Nero's dark reign, in a closely guarded room in the palace, a man tells his story.

Neophytus, Imperial dream interpreter seer, has returned to Rome from Judea in flight from the death grip of an ancient cult. He has not returned alone, for his nightmares have followed him into the palace. The Acts of the Apostates is an odyssey undertaken by mystics, charlatans and sorcerers through occult mysteries and madness.

£**6.99**   ISBN 0 946626 46 4   272pp   B Format

The Acts of the Apostates is one of the many works of contemporary fiction inspired by the literature and history of the Romans and we include a few pages to give the flavour of the novel and as an act of homage to its predecessors.

The Acts of the Apostates (p8–11)

When the play was over, and Canace's incestuous bastard dutifully thrown to the hunting dogs, Nero, red faced and smiling, took up his lyre and began to sing. His energy was boundless. Actors who performed with him complained privately that they were ready to drop from exhaustion before Nero worked up a decent sweat. He sang through the whole afternoon and on into the evening. It was typical of him to forget about the time. The flagging audience tried to keep up their enthusiasm for the Emperor's undeniable vocal talents, but after about six hours the heat and overcrowding inside the theatre was beginning to take its effect. Most of them had no interest in music or drama anyway. They attended to court the Emperor's goodwill. And naturally no one would leave before the performance finished, for fear of giving offence.

Gradually people began to faint and had to be carried from the auditorium by the Emperor's guards and slaves. Several people saw their opportunity and feigned unconsciousness as a means of escape.

Finally Nero laid aside his lyre. The relieved spectators realised that at last the entertainment was over and burst into thunderous applause, which for one awful moment threatened to bring Nero bounding back on stage for another encore. Everyone rose stiffly and hurried out into the streets.

At once the Emperor began to dash about in a panic. He had not planned that his performance should last so long, he said, but clearly the audience were so enraptured it would have been unfair to deprive them.

'But now I am behind myself,' he cried, 'and there are urgent matters to attend to.'

'There are, Caesar!' Epaphroditus stepped forward resolutely. 'First, we must discuss the grain shortage . . .'

'*Not that!*' Nero glared at him. 'I mean that now I shall be late for rehearsals.'

Epaphroditus did not flinch, nor betray any sign of emotion save that his face turned puce. Nero grinned.

'I have become so absorbed lately with affairs of state that my performances are becoming irregular. I must be dedicated. My public deserve nothing less.'

To avoid the slow and weary business of making his way through the crowds outside, Nero walked by way of a *cryptoporticus*, a subterranean passageway that led to an entrance hall of the palace. This was a rebuilt section of an old network of passages mostly destroyed by the great fire in Rome four years earlier. It was gloomy, and a musty odour hung in the air. The stucco reliefs of elegant pavilions, nymphs and cupids that covered the walls did little to lighten the sense of oppression. As the Emperor, with his party of guards and attendants, made his way along it, Epaphroditus recalled that it had been somewhere nearby, more than twenty-five years earlier, that Nero's uncle, the Emperor Gaius Caligula, met his death. Another Caesar who had broken with the Senate, lured here after a morning in the theatre by a group of assassins – some of them members of his own Guard – who leapt upon him from all sides and hacked him to death. At one point, so the story went, his murderers, believing him to be finished, backed away from his body. But Caligula had raised his head, his jaw half severed from his face, and bellowed: '*I am not yet dead!*' A peculiarly stupid thing to say in Epaphroditus' view. But then, Caligula had always been over critical of his Guard. It was said throughout the city that Caligula's ghost roamed these gloomy cloisters by night, repeating the dreadful screams he had made choking out his savage life.

Epaphroditus glanced at the Emperor. He was pale faced, his heavy, handsome features frowning nervously. His blond curls were lank and he seemed to be sweating even more profusely than he had on stage. Clearly he too was aware of the stories that circulated about this place, and combined with the eerie effect of torchlight, they were making him uneasy. When his reign had begun, Nero's appalling mother Agrippina — who had schemed, seduced, committed incest and murdered that she might make her son Emperor and rule through him — had reminded him of the harrowing details of her brother Caligula's demise whenever he had shown independence of spirit, intimating that if Nero was foolish enough not to be guided by her experience in all things, a similar fate might befall him. Nero had never been able to forget her words. Because of them he had developed an obsessive terror of assassination. At this moment, the ghosts of both Caligula and Agrippina rose to haunt him. Well, that was no bad thing, Epaphroditus reflected. A healthy scare was perhaps just what the Emperor needed to make him start taking the present threats against him seriously. Nero quickened his pace.

Back at the palace, Nero did not join the company for dinner, but went straight away to rehearse. A special diet, he said, was most necessary to a singer, whose vocal chords might suffer from the wrong kinds of food.

Throughout the banquet, Neophytus and Epaphroditus spoke little and ate less, each caught within their own private concerns. In silence they reclined upon dining couches while handsome slaves in short white tunics bathed guests' hands and feet in rose scented iced water, and an orchestra played vigorous excerpts from the Emperor's own musical compositions. Little girls moved to and fro amongst the diners, sprinkling exotic perfumes while epicene actors circled giant pillars in the gloom beyond the torchlit tables and couches, their voices made resonant in the great chamber while they recited verse — Nero's verse — to accompany his music.

When toast and libation to gods and Emperor were done, there began the procession of dinner courses: oysters from Britain, lobster and mullet, fried calves' testicles, thrushes in garlic, pâté of lark tongues, every variety of game bird, honeyed dormice, sows' udders in pepper sauce, roasted boar stuffed with spiced mushrooms, and much more. Epaphroditus nibbled at some quail encased in an orange jelly then abandoned the effort as he felt indigestion begin to rise. Neophytus too ate barely a thing, but drank heavy quantities of Nero's vintage Falernian wine while staring blankly at the floor. Epaphroditus leaned towards him finally. The matter must be broached again. He must be persistent.

'Sometimes he invites leading citizens to banquets so he can perform for them. When he does you can bet a brass sesterce to a gold talent that it will be something obscene. Not long ago he played the part of a bride. Some actor was the bridegroom. They recited the marriage vows in all solemnity, then retired behind a curtain where he imitated the squeals of a girl being deflowered. And his going about with the pretty eunuch done up like Queen Dido of Carthage doesn't help matters much. Have you seen the walls about the city? There is offensive graffiti everywhere.'

'Yes, I've seen some,' Neophytus nodded. 'There was one verse outside the Temple of Saturn about Nero and Sporus the eunuch. The punchline was the eunuch has nothing to look forward to, but plenty to look back on. Quite witty, I thought.'